The Commitment Factor

THE COMMITMENT FACTOR

Carrol Bruce

BROADMAN PRESS
Nashville, Tennessee

© Copyright 1984 ● Broadman Press
All rights reserved
4255-41
ISBN: 0-8054-5541-8
Dewey Decimal Classification: 254
Subject Heading: NEW CHURCHES
Library of Congress Catalog Card Number: 84-5005
Printed in the United States of America

Library of Congress Cataloging in Publication Data

Bruce, Carrol, 1929,-
 The commitment factor.

 1. Fort Foote Baptist Church (Oxon Hill, Md.)
2. Church development, New.   I. Title.
BX6480.0924B7   1984   286′.175251   84-5005
ISBN 0-8054-5541-8

To **Frances**
for her partnership in the work, and
to **Herbert** and **Margaret Bruce**, my parents,
for preparing me to do this kind of work

Acknowledgment

I acknowledge with gratitude *Joel T. Land* of the Home Mission Board of the Southern Baptist Convention for his suggestions and help in preparing my manuscript for publication by Broadman Press.

Foreword

Carrol Bruce has written a book that needs to be read today. Twelve special people came together for a time and experienced a miracle: the birth of a new church. Twenty-five years later Bruce interviewed those people to see what difference the church made in their lives.

We need to read this story in the middle of Bold Mission Thrust. Bruce shows that boldness is not waiting to start fifteen thousand new churches until the Home Mission Board can collect enough money. Boldness is going ahead to meet needs one by one, until suddenly a church is started. Bruce believes a church is born the moment a pastor or layperson believes it can be. He tells how the money, the people, and thousands of details miraculously happened as twelve modern disciples acted on faith.

We need to read this story to remind us that seminary students and young men, even in their first pastorates, can start new churches as well as older professionals. Bruce demonstrates how the Lord honors all efforts to glorify his name even if they begin in a roadside fruit stand.

This book honors the sacrificial service of bivocational pastors who stretch the most out of every day. It honors those who pursue their calling even if they have to pay their own salary. It honors those who don't wait to serve until just the right opportunity comes along, those who are willing to make something splendid out of whatever opportunity is available.

The story of the Fort Foote Baptist Church is both unique and classic. Unique in that it only happened once but classic in that the same dynamics happen in almost every new-church start. New pastors, seminary classes, bivocational pastors, sponsoring-church pastors, and anyone else interested in starting new churches will be inspired and taught by this case history.

Joel Land, my associate, has also written an interpretation chapter to isolate the repeatable elements of Carrol Bruce's story. Land answers the haunting questions: What made this experience successful? and How does one go about starting a new church? Carrol Bruce's twelve disciples live again wherever a new church is born.

JACK REDFORD
Atlanta, Georgia

CONTENTS

1
The Draft

Only God could produce the web of circumstances that placed me on the front steps of Congress Heights Baptist Church one Sunday morning in time to hear a passing conversation that changed my life and the lives of hundreds of others. Those critical moments ultimately led to the start of a new church at Fort Foote, Maryland.

I was on those steps only because God, when it suited his purpose, could get a reluctant ordained minister drafted into the armed services during peacetime. How I got to Washington, D.C., was a big surprise to me, but God's drafting had really been going on in my life for quite some time. Who knows when God first begins preparing a person for a call to the ministry?

The crisis which ultimately brought me to the Washington, D.C., area started in Cincinnati, Ohio, soon after Frances and I were married in 1952. During our two and one-half years in Cincinnati, I worked as a research chemist for the Drackett Company; Frances worked as a secretary for the International Chemical Corporation.

In the summer of 1954, I took a job with Armour and Company; we moved to Somerset, Kentucky. My work took me over twenty-one southeastern counties of Kentucky. In September of that year, our daughter, Anna, was born. Frances was kept busy being a new mother. My new job kept me away from home on the average of about two nights a week.

In Cincinnati, we had been very active in the Lockland Baptist Church which had about three thousand members and offered us great opportunities for service. In Somerset, we joined the Calvary Baptist Church which had about two hundred members but also offered plenty of opportunity for us to participate in the life of the church.

We settled into a new life in Kentucky, but I was still not satisfied. This lack of satisfaction bothered me a lot, especially during the evenings when I was away from home. I liked my work, but I wanted something different. I wasn't sure what it was, but I did give considerable thought and prayer to the suggestions that my last two pastors had made. I suppose it was because of my love for the church that caused both of them to suggest that I consider going into full-time church-related work. At that time, that could only be interpreted as becoming a preacher.

I had been taught that God calls persons into the ministry by exerting so much pressure that the person had to respond. In other words, there had to be an unmistakable and unavoidable call from God. I was interested, but the call just was not that clear. So, the struggle within me continued for the next several months. The more I thought about it, which was most of my free time, the less satisfaction I was getting from my work with Armour and Company.

Finally, in a small motel room in Pineville, Kentucky, out of desperation, I made a commitment to God to go into the ministry. After talking it over with Frances and getting her approval, I announced publicly to the Calvary Baptist Church that I had accepted God's call to be a preacher. When Frances approved and I announced it to the church, there was no turning back.

About six weeks later, even though I had no seminary training, I was called to be the pastor of the East Union Baptist Church. The church was just a few miles from where I was raised. I accepted that call, prepared to leave Armour and Company, and made arrangements to be ordained by the Mount Pisgah Baptist Church where I had been a member until going to college. All of this happened within a few weeks.

Everything was going so well for us that both Frances and I felt very strongly that we had made the right decision. The East Union Church had a nice parsonage, the congregation was large enough to give us a salary that would enable me to enroll in The Southern Baptist Theological Seminary in Louisville, Kentucky, which was within easy commuting distance from the church. I was ordained, resigned from Armour and Company, and set a date to move into the parsonage. I was already commuting from Somerset to the East Union Church each Sunday to preach.

While all this was happening, I received a notice from my local draft board. I had not heard from them since registering for the military draft at age eighteen. The notice was for a preinduction physical examination. I had entered college when barely seventeen, enrolled in the Reserve Officers Training Corps for four years, and was commissioned as an officer in the Air Force upon graduation. That was in 1950, the beginning of the Korean War. The commission was good for five years, and the agreement with the Air Force was that two years of that time would be spent on active duty.

Normally, the call for active duty came immediately upon graduation from college. The only exception was if the officer continued his education in a graduate school, which I did. I finished my graduate course just prior to getting married in 1952. Even though I went ahead and got a job, I fully expected to be called to active duty at that time. When the call to active duty didn't come after a reasonable waiting time, Frances and I decided I should request it in order to get the active-duty time over with before we had children.

I made the official request to the Air Force Records Center and kept a copy of the request. The letter of request never came back and neither did a call to active duty. I was really not anxious to get into the Korean War, so I just left the responsibility for getting me into active duty up to the Air Force. I was obligated and had officially requested it, but the Air Force didn't respond.

I received my draft notice about one month before my five-year commission as an Air Force officer was to expire. Of course, the Korean War had long since ended. And for the first time in many years, there was no declared national emergency.

Upon receiving notice from the local draft board, I immediately went before them and showed proof that I was a duly commissioned officer and was still awaiting a call to active duty. The draft board informed me that unless I was in fact on active duty I was still eligible to be drafted into military service and that was what the board was going to do. Even though there was no national emergency, the draft laws were still in effect.

The East Union Baptist Church, along with the Baptist association of forty-five churches, made an appeal to the draft board to exempt me from military service. They pointed out that I had been ordained and was just beginning my service as a pastor, but it was to no avail. The board gave me one option to being drafted and that was to be called to active duty in the Air Force.

For me, being a lieutenant in the Air Force was better than being a private in the Army for reasons too numerous to mention. The only problem in exercising my option was that I only had two days to do it. I had passed the preinduction physical examination while the attempt to get an exemption was being made by the churches. The day I was to be drafted into the Army was the same day that my Air Force officer's commission was to expire.

Knowing this, I called the Air Force Records Center to

report my plight and ask for a quick call to active duty. I reminded them of my letter of request some three years earlier, but they seemed neither to have a record of it nor a record that I was ever commissioned. Since I had a record of both, I threatened to contact my congressman. Believe it or not, they immediately found both of my lost records in the proper place in the Air Force Records Center.

The Air Force had responded to my earlier request by calling another person with the same name as mine to active duty. The serial number was different, but the file clerk had not bothered to check that.

The final result of my phone call to the records center was that the Air Force called my draft board that day and was given six weeks to get me assigned to active duty. This they did by sending me to Bolling Air Force Base. I fully expected to be released from the Air Force in a very short time. I began to work toward that end, as did the East Union Baptist Church and the Baptist association of that county.

At that point, I felt being the pastor of the East Union Baptist Church was the only way that I could keep the commitment to God that I had made back in Pineville, Kentucky, a few months before. I felt it was right for me to be a pastor rather than a lieutenant in the Air Force. In short, to accept the call to be a preacher was so special that I felt it totally subordinated any other area of responsibility.

Again, in retrospect, I can see that my attempt to be released from the Air Force was wrong. Now I can see how being in the Air Force was the best way of keeping my commitment to God. But I certainly did not know that at that time.

My assignment at Bolling was with the Office of Special Investigation, which was called the F.B.I. of the Air Force. After security clearance and six months special training in a school operated by the F.B.I., I would be a special agent.

This all seemed so contradictory to my commitment to be a preacher that it was almost like a big practical joke.

When my superiors would read my resume, they would invariably call me in and inquire about my ordination. They not only felt it hard to believe that I was there but weren't sure they wanted me there. Apparently, they had some reservation about a Baptist minister investigating a criminal case. So, I expected my stay at Bolling Air Force Base to be a very temporary one. I wanted to be released from active duty, my church wanted me back as pastor, forty-five churches in a Baptist association had requested it, and the people I had been assigned to work under did not really want me. And, most of all, it just didn't seem to me that God would let me lose two years of service and seminary training.

I was so sure of returning to my Kentucky pastorate that Frances and Anna remained there and I lived in the bachelor officer's quarters on the base. We had six weeks in which to move family and furniture, so we waited thinking that we would just have to move right back.

After all efforts to get me released had been made, the word from the directorate for O.S.I. in the Pentagon came that the commitment that I had made when entering the R.O.T.C. program in college would have to be kept. That commitment was to serve on active duty for two years. The letter stated that there was one way that I could be released and that was to declare myself a conscientious objector, which I was not.

With this final word from the Air Force, I sent my letter of resignation to the church. Frances and Anna came to Washington, D.C., and a new phase of our lives began. We moved into an apartment and attended the Congress Heights Baptist Church the first Sunday that we were together. We liked the people, the pastor, all the programs we knew about, and began attending regularly. I was still angry about the turn of events and felt reluctant to tell people that I was an ordained minister because it didn't quite seem legitimate now that I was in training to be an O.S.I. officer in the Air Force.

Then the turning point came. The next Sunday as we were leaving, two young men, one going up the steps and one going down, stopped to chat. The one leaving the church asked the one arriving, "Where have you been?" He answered, "I have been out to Fort Foote to conduct a worship service. Only two people showed up so I'm not going back anymore."

At that point, I interrupted the conversation. "Pardon me. Can you tell me more about Fort Foote?" There on the steps of the Congress Heights Baptist Church, the young man explained why he had been to Fort Foote to conduct a worship service. "Earlier in the summer, the young people of the church and Joe Strother held a tent revival in the Fort Foote community with the intention of starting a new church. Not many people live in the community and the attendance at the meetings was small. One young married couple was baptized, but they seem to be about the only ones interested in continuing the services on a regular basis. Today, they were the only ones there."

As reluctant as I had been to say it, I finally said, "I am an ordained Baptist minister. I would be interested in learning more about the Fort Foote situation." With this, we went inside the church to meet the pastor. We had spoken to him at the close of each service but had not talked with him at any length.

A. Lincoln Smith was a very warm, friendly person with more enthusiasm for starting a new church than I had ever seen. As I now look back on my relationship and experiences with him over that six-year period, his ways were not always my ways, but he was as committed to his call to the ministry as anyone I have ever known. He was always supportive and encouraging.

The result of the meeting that day was that Congress Heights Baptist Church was ready to start a new church in the Fort Foote community. I volunteered to be the first pastor.

2
The Beginning

With encouragement from the church, Frances and I decided we would ask Barbara and Bucky Dalton, the young couple who had been baptized at the tent revival, about holding a prayer meeting and Bible study in their home the following Sunday evening.

The Daltons agreed to let us meet in their home. That first Sunday evening in September 1955, there were eleven people in attendance, including the four small Dalton children. We continued for a few weeks in that home with usually about the same number of people in attendance. It was an opportunity for me to do something within my calling while in the Air Force, but not much progress was being made toward starting a new church.

It was evident that a public place was needed in order to get more people to attend. We invited people, but they did not come. I began to inquire about a public building that we could use. We all agreed that this should be our first priority.

The Fort Foote community was only about a five-to ten-minute drive from the D.C. boundary line, but there were still very few people living there. The name Fort Foote came from General Foote who had commanded a Revolutionary military fort facing Alexandria, Virginia, across the Potomac River. Most of the people who lived in the community had been there for several years, but traveled into D.C. or Oxon Hill for worship. Some of the newcomers to the area lived in two small housing developments. One was Fort

Foote Terrace, with about ten or twelve houses, where the Daltons lived; and the other was called Kirby Hills, with about fifty houses. These houses were much smaller and less expensive than what was to come later when the Washington area began to expand in that direction. But at that time, there were no public buildings in the immediate Fort Foote community except a grocery store and a garage.

It appeared that what we believed to be our greatest need in starting a church could not be met in that community. Then one day as I was driving through the community, I noticed a little building sitting about fifty feet off Fort Foote Road. It was on the property of a longtime chicken farmer who was in the process of retiring. The property included not only the little building but also twenty-five acres which had several chicken houses and a feed storage building. I did not know what it had been used for, but stopped to inquire.

Jay Green came to the farmhouse door when I knocked. He appeared to be about sixty-five years old. He said he had lived in that house most of his life and worked in the chicken and egg business with his father and brother. Both father and brother had died, and he was now the sole owner of the property.

I told him, "I'm Carrol Bruce. I'm here to start a church in the community and need a building other than a home for a place to hold meetings. Since yours are the only buildings offering that possibility, I wonder if one might be available to us?"

He removed his pipe, chuckled a little, and asked me to repeat what I had just said. This time I was a little more specific, "Can we use the feed storage building?" It was larger and looked to be in better repair.

He could not believe that I was making such a request. "No, you can't use the larger building because I still use it for storage space. The other building is an old roadside stand where we used to sell fruits and vegetables. In my wildest imagination, I cannot believe you would want that building for a church meeting place."

Mr. Green told me, "I have never been a member of any church and have not gone to any kind of church meeting for thirty-five years. But, your request is very interesting because thirty-five years ago my father built a concrete block building on the opposite corner of his farm at the request of another minister, whose name I forget, to start a new church.

"The project didn't last long, and the building was converted into the country store, which you see over there. Your church probably won't last either, but, if you want it, you can have it."

The road-side stand building was ten feet by twenty feet with a roof over three walls and a half. The half was the open window through which the fruits and vegetables had been displayed. That window was still open and the only floor was the ground.

We visited for a couple of hours sharing our backgrounds and parted with Mr. Green's thinking that my kind was doomed to failure in the church business and probably not any good for the Air Force either. Whatever he thought about our little group's endeavor, I was grateful for our first public meeting place.

It was in the fall so the building would have to have a floor, the open window closed, and a stove installed as soon as possible. I inquired in the area for a carpenter and was told that there was one who lived in the woods. When I went to his home, a woman came to the door and said, "Yes, Mr. Bryant is home. Tip, come here. Somebody wants you."

He said, "Yes, I'm a carpenter. What do you want?"

"We need help to do the repair work on the fruit stand for a church," I answered. He was startled, but agreed to help me. I learned later that the woman who came to the door was his common-law wife and neither of them had been to church in their lives enough to speak about.

I don't remember where we got the materials, but Bucky Dalton, Tip Bryant, and I put the building in sufficient condition to have our first meeting within a few days. We now had a public meeting place and began with new vigor to invite others to join us in worship at 11:00 AM and 7:30 PM on Sundays. Our meeting place was different; but, strange as it may seem, our little group had a certain pride in it.

Of course, the people in the community who had been traveling into the main Washington area to worship continued to do so. It was almost unthinkable for an established churchgoer to accept a roadside fruit stand as a place of worship.

So, the only prospects we had were people who were not professing Christians or who had not been active in church for many years. We made sure they were invited. The invitation was always by direct word of mouth from me or one of our group.

When free from Air Force duties, I was always available to follow up on contacts made by others. Often, the contacts were people in some kind of crisis situation. My work as the pastor was primarily responding to needs of friends and relatives of church members.

Our unlikely meeting place, with an Air Force officer as the pastor, did attract people who had never attended church or who had not attended for a long time. Most did not want to go to an ordinary building and be a part of a regular congregation because of the chaotic lives they lived. Not all who came were in this category but many of the early members were. Some were like Mrs. Snead, a very devout Christian and church member, who came hoping to get some of her family back into church. She felt they would more likely be willing to come to a place like we had than where she had been attending. Mrs. Snead and others in her family became stalwarts in the church that was developing.

A police officer who lived near our church started attending. One Sunday he asked me, "Where did you get this fellow who was a visitor with us today?"

I said, "I didn't get him from anywhere. He came with a regular attender."

The officer said, "I can't believe I'm seeing that man in church. How many times have I seen him in jail?"

Another time our offering was considerably larger than it had been before. We all wondered about the increase. I learned later that the extra amount had been given by a visitor who had won the money in a crap game the night before. It is significant to note that people like these became founders of the church that was developing.

Our group continued to increase in the next few months until we had as many as forty people attending. The building was only ten by twenty and had a stove and piano in it. There wasn't enough space for forty chairs. One Sunday we folded up the chairs, put them outside, and all stood for the service. That day, whatever we lacked in facilities we had in closeness.

Our building was limited in many ways other than space. One limitation was that the building was not wired for electricity. One of the men installed a lighting fixture and connected a line to Mr. Green's house, which was about a hundred feet away. When the meeting was over, the electric cord was unplugged and rolled up until the next meeting. During the evening meeting, it just lay on the ground and at times latecomers who didn't know about the electrical arrangement would drive over the wire, unplugging it and leaving us in darkness until someone went to the house and plugged it in again.

In spite of the limited facilities of our unusual meeting place, we had established the fact that we were serious about building a church in that community. It was now time for us to think in terms of a permanent church congregation, not just a little group of mostly unaffiliated church people meeting to worship.

3
The First Twelve Members

The Congress Heights Baptist Church had decided to start a church in the Fort Foote area when they held the first tent revival. They continued as our sponsoring church and supported us as much as they could through encouragement and prayer. Actually, Fort Foote could have a pastor only because of my Air Force salary. The sponsoring church could do little more because they were expanding rapidly and were in a large building program of their own.

I mention this in order to introduce the first twelve members of the Fort Foote Church. In the Baptist structure, the beginning group is known as a mission. Technically, members of the mission are members of the sponsoring church until they are "duly organized into a Baptist church"

From the beginning, I did not like to use the word *mission* in reference to our group. I believed a group was a church by virtue of its relationship to God as revealed in Jesus Christ and its ministry and not by organizational structure. Also, to be called a mission was to be given second-rate church status which I felt to be a hindrance to the development of a church in the community.

In my mind the twelve whom I am going to tell about were the first members of the Fort Foote Baptist Church, even though we were known by the mother church as a mission. The sponsoring pastor and I had long discussions about this, which usually ended in some kind of compromise. In keeping with the Baptist method, we asked all who joined to go before the Congress Heights congregation for membership. Twelve of us did that in late 1955. Each who joined after that was put on an official church roll and technically became a member of the Congress Heights Baptist Church until the organizational service for Fort Foote Baptist Church in 1958. However, none of us thought of ourselves as members of Congress Heights; rather we were members of Fort Foote. Fort Foote Baptist Church was chartered with eighty-one members.

However, there were only twelve in 1955 who went before the Congress Heights Baptist Church to be recognized as a part of the Congress Heights Baptist Church meeting in the Fort Foote community. These are the people I call the first members.

They seemed so biblical, like Jesus' twelve disciples. Only Jesus would have called together such a varied group. We often thought of ourselves as walking with Jesus on the shores of the Potomac, trying to do what he would do. These twelve disciples set the character and direction of the church in the beginning. So let me introduce them to you:

Disciple 1:	Barbara Dalton
Disciple 2:	Harold "Bucky" Dalton
Disciple 3:	Lilly Bowen
Disciple 4:	Marie "Cookie" Mitchell
Disciple 5:	Kenny Bowen
Disciple 6:	Dolly Van Wormer
Disciple 7:	Dolly Sherman
Disciple 8:	Gary Sherman
Disciple 9:	Sara Redman
Disciple 10:	Maudice Roberts
Disciple 11:	Frances Bruce
Disciple 12:	Carrol Bruce

Disciple 1 and Disciple 2: Barbara and Bucky Dalton

Barbara and Bucky had four children ranging in age from one to five years. The two youngest were twins. The family was living in Fort Foote Terrace, one of the two small housing developments in the community that I mentioned earlier. I don't know Barbara's background, though I recall meeting her mother during the time Barbara was attending the church. Bucky and his father operated the Fort Foote Foundry, so I got to know his family very well.

I do not know why Barbara and Bucky attended the tent revival, except that it was near their house and they received a personal invitation. They told me that there had been personal crises in their lives from time to time, so I suspect they were looking for the kind of help the church had to offer. During that tent revival, they both committed their lives to Christ and were baptized by Al Smith, the pastor of Congress Heights Baptist Church.

We had first met in their home for the prayer and Bible study meetings. They had both been faithful in attending and inviting their friends after we moved the meetings out of their house. From the beginning, their family's contacts in the community brought many people into the church.

Bucky was a rather quiet member but always available and willing to do any physical work that was needed. He was a great help because we were, in the truest sense of the words, a "do-it-yourself church." When he wasn't able to do a job himself, he either got someone who could or referred us to someone.

Barbara, even though the mother of four young children, rarely missed a service and always had the name of someone for me to contact as a prospect for our church or who wanted and needed some help from the church. Also, she was the first treasurer of the church. Those who wanted to give money gave it to her at the morning worship service. She

kept it until the evening service when sometimes there was
a little added. Then it was taken either Sunday night or
Monday morning for bank deposit. Barbara kept the record
of the amount that came in, which never got above one
hundred dollars per week in the earlier days.

Bucky and Barbara were active for about two years. Then
during a brief separation, Barbara stopped attending and
Bucky stopped a short time later. They never came back to
the church while I was pastor but continued to live in the
community. Barbara had given up the treasurer's job some
time earlier as it had begun to involve too much work in
keeping the records and getting the money deposited.

I saw them often and encouraged them to come back to
church, but they never did. Bucky told me later that they
continued to have periods of short separations and finally
separated permanently. I saw him just a few days before
writing this, and he was living with his mother. Their children are grown and living in various places in the Washington area.

When I was back for the twentieth anniversary of the
church, a young man in his twenties came up to me and said
he was Bucky and Barbara's son. He said he was one of the
babies who cried during services in the first little building.
He was married and active in a local church at the time of
the twentieth-anniversary service. I was always saddened by
the fact that Bucky and Barbara had stopped attending the
church, but I had a very warm and satisfying feeling to know
that this son, and perhaps others of their children whom I
don't know about, had been influenced by their participation in the very beginning of the church. Bucky and Barbara
were the only original members who later dropped out of
the church, but both were vital in getting the church
started.

The First Twelve Members

Barbara Dalton Speaks

My background is much like that of any other person from a broken home where both parents are alcoholics. As a child, I never stayed in one place very long and was usually a ward of the court, placed in homes of strangers.

After running away from the last school I was placed in, I found myself with my mother again. I started attending the Fifth Baptist Church in southwest Washington, D.C.

Reverend Briggs was a very understanding man. I had been familiar with the teachings of Christ in my very early childhood. So I accepted Christ and was baptized when I was twelve years old. Shortly thereafter I moved to Georgia to live with my oldest sister and did not affiliate with a church.

Two marriages and four children later, in my mid-twenties, I was living at Fort Foote Village in Fort Foote, Maryland. Three girls came to my house one day and told me they were going to hold a revival on the corner lot, sponsored by the Congress Heights Baptist Church and invited me to attend.

After the church people got their tent set up, I decided to go and see what it was like, hoping they wouldn't be screaming and fainting like they did at a little building one of my aunts had taken me to when I was small. That nearly scared me to death. I know now that was a different religion. But I was small and had no idea we had more than one faith, being told and believing we only had one God.

The third night I attended the tent revival, Brother Joe Strother was preaching. He really knew how to get the message across. It seemed as if he had singled me out and the entire sermon was directed at me. I felt myself under strong conviction, a feeling I have never experienced before or since.

After the revival, I started going to Congress Heights Baptist Church. My husband, Bucky, would take care of the twins, Donald and Debbie, and the two older boys, Brian and Alan.

I can't remember who suggested the prayer meeting. I know Carrol

Bruce was involved and Joe did a lot of leg work to provide the names of people who might be interested.

Mrs. Bowen, a long-time friend and second mother to me, started having prayer meetings at her home, and I offered my living room on Wednesday nights. Jay Green offered to let us have services in the little vegetable stand near his house on the side of the road. It was really small, but there were so few of us that it was plenty big enough at the time. As more people started coming to the vegetable stand, Uncle Jay let us use his feed house, as it was much larger. Uncle Jay, as I called him, wasn't really my uncle, but I used that term of affection, as did others. Everyone who knew him loved him and his sister-in-law Aunt Dolly Van Wormer.

I think that was the happiest period in my life, having Christ in my life and being part of the little church, watching the men paint and fix things. Reverend Bruce was right in there working with them. Frances, his wife, was such a pleasant, gentle person. Sara Redman was a great inspiration to me at that time. She played the piano. Of course, I knew Aunt Dolly and Mrs. Bowen would be there for me, if I needed to talk.

I taught the little children for a while and took the collection home to count and write down and check attendance. Carolyn Alexander and I would usually take care of the nursery at the feed house. It was really a good feeling to attend church and listen to Reverend Bruce preach.

Somehow I let myself slip away from the church. I would still send the children, Marla and Dwayne.

I've been divorced for some time and don't go to church now, but I'm very thankful the church is there. That is where all my children received their basic religious training. I believe that once Christ is instilled in children's hearts they will never stray too far away from God's Word.

I will always be thankful for the revival at Fort Foote many years ago and for the men and women who worked and prayed so hard to build the church that they have now. I am also thankful that God let me be a part of that small group that helped lay the foundation.

Disciple 3: Lilly Bowen

Lilly Bowen was probably in her late forties when she first attended the prayer and Bible study meetings in the Dalton's home. She was the kind of person who seemed to attract needy people to herself. There was always some person at her house who had come for help. Usually, help was a place to stay while a crisis passed. George, her husband, never came to church, and I never knew him well. Apparently he was at least sympathetic with her benevolence toward everyone. Even when she wasn't feeling well or things weren't going well for her, she was able to smile or laugh. She obviously never had much money but managed to buy food for a lot of people, as well as give some money to the church. When we resigned from the church, she gave us a rather expensive mixer that we still use. Knowing her financial situation, that mixer is one of the most meaningful gifts we ever received.

Lilly, like the Daltons, knew most of the people who had lived a long time in the community, especially the handicapped or "down and out." She had told me about Tip Bryant, the carpenter, and many others who later became part of the church. She had more influence among many of the people in the community than anyone else simply because she had helped so many of them in one way or another.

She told me about a family of eleven children who lived in an abandoned-looking house near the church. The house was back in the woods between the church and the river and could not be seen unless approached by the narrow dirt road leading to it. At Lilly's request, I visited the family and got most of the children started in Sunday School, even though the parents never came. It was a large family that was very poor largely because of an irresponsible father. He drank up whatever income he could get from working on the rare occasions when he was sober. Lilly knew about that family and tried to help them.

Once when I was passing the Bowen's house, Lilly and another member of the church were standing in the yard, which was always filled with old cars and dogs but no grass. I stopped and joined what was simply a neighborly chat. The lady visiting with Lilly was much younger, more educated, and certainly had a lot more money. But they were greatly enjoying one another's company. They were in Lilly's yard, but their common ground was their faith in Christ and their church. A scene like that gave me enough encouragement in church work to last for several days and to keep the church related to the perspective that all are the same under God.

When Lilly died less than a year ago, many people attending her funeral were the recipients of her benevolence, which said more about her than the two preachers who conducted the funeral service.

Disciple 4: Marie "Cookie" Mitchell

At that first meeting in the Dalton home, Lilly brought with her a little blonde girl who was about ten years old. She introduced her to me as "Cookie." I thought she was Lilly's daughter, but shortly learned that Cookie was her foster child. At a very young age, Cookie had been brought to Lilly for baby-sitting and her real parents never came back to get her. As far as Lilly was concerned, Cookie was her child.

Perhaps as much as anyone else, Cookie grew up in the Fort Foote Baptist Church. She was the youngest of the original twelve members and attended regularly, as least as long as I was there. She may have been the one who profited most from the church, as she was the youngest member for some time.

She married at an early age, and I didn't see her after I left the church until she called and asked that I participate in

Lilly's funeral service. As Lilly had accepted the role of responsible mother, Cookie accepted the role of responsible daughter. Observing this was evidence that basic commitments result in good happenings.

Cookie Mitchell Coggins Speaks

I was taken in by Mary L. and George W. Bowen when I was seventeen months old. Mom told me why she took me. It was because she loved me. My real parents are still alive, and they would never let Mom and Dad adopt me.

I have gone all my life with the nickname of Cookie. I am the oldest of seven children of my real parents. I do get to see them and my real brothers and sisters. I also have a foster brother whose name is Kenny. Mom and Dad Bowen adopted him when he was very young. Mom said I should know and see my real parents, so they would take me over to see them. I love my real parents but not as much as I do Mom and Dad.

I grew up at 7351 Fort Foote Road, Oxon Hill, Maryland. Later the address changed to 8709 Fort Foote Road. I went to Oxon Hill Elementary School and Oxon Hill Junior High School.

Mom and I started going to Oxon Hill Baptist Church. I was about five or six years old when we started to church. I was saved at Oxon Hill Church and so was Mom. Dad didn't go to church with us, but he would take us.

Mom and I longed to have a church close by so we could walk to services. A few of the people who lived in the neighborhood started having prayer meetings in the Dalton's home. Then Mom and some of the people started having church services in Uncle Jay's fruit stand. Soon we had so many people that we started meeting in Uncle Jay's feed house. I think I was about nine or ten years old. I think we started out with about twelve people, and we grew to the church we are now.

I can remember when I was young how I loved to talk about Jesus and tell people how much I loved him and how much love I had to give for my Lord. I was taught by my mom that you trusted and obeyed all of God's words. Mom had a warm and loving feeling for people. She would witness to people about what the Lord had done for her.

Fort Foote Baptist Church will always have a special place in my heart because of my mother and Reverend Bruce and his family who worked and prayed to get our church built. And because of the teaching and love from all the people who started our church, and the teacher who taught me about God and his love.

I do want to thank Reverend Bruce and his family and also Reverend Leonard, the second pastor after Reverend Bruce left for Japan, for all the teaching and talks and Bible study we had. And I want to thank my mother and Pastor Bruce for the love and devotion which made me the person I am today: a very loving and thankful person with love in my heart who helped to start a church.

Disciple 5: Kenny Bowen

Kenny was not with Lilly and Cookie at that first meeting but came soon after we moved into our first building. He was about seventeen years old at that time. He, like Cookie, had come to the Bowens by the baby-sitting, foster-child route. I don't know when or under what circumstances he first came to them or was adopted, but I am sure it was at a very early age. I never heard his real parents mentioned during all the years of close contact that I had with the Bowen family.

Kenny was beginning to get a rather undesirable reputation in the community due to the way he drove "souped-up" cars. According to Lilly, when he first came to our church, he was either in some trouble relating to his cardriving, or just getting out of it. Kenny continued to attend church regularly and became one of the original twelve members. He was the only male teenager in that group, which may have been his main contribution in interesting certain female prospects for our church.

I had to be away at a time when my wife needed someone

to take her to Upper Marlboro to take the test to get her driver's license. Kenny was the person she asked to take her. He was surprised that she would ask him but graciously consented to do it.

Disciple 6: Dolly Van Wormer

Mrs. Van Wormer came to the first meeting we had in the converted fruit stand. She was in her sixties and had been married to Mr. Green's half-brother. Since Mr. Green had never married, he lived with the Van Wormers, or maybe it was that the Van Wormers had lived with him. Whatever the arrangement, it continued even after Mr. Van Wormer died.

Mrs. Van Wormer and the two grandchildren who lived with her were members of the Oxon Hill Baptist Church but did not attend regularly. Since our meeting place was in her yard, she decided to attend. She was a very friendly person, always ready to laugh. Her main interests were Dolly and Gary Sherman, the two grandchildren who lived with her. Dolly, who was about ninteen years old, was four when she moved in with her grandmother. Gary was born while his mother was living there, so he had never lived anywhere else. In fact, their mother told me that Gary never really knew his father and that Dolly was probably too young when he left them for her to remember him. I never spoke to either Gary or Dolly about their father and only once to their mother about him.

I do know that Mrs. Van Wormer had the responsibility of raising Gary and Dolly and was doing her best as a sixty-year-old grandmother with limited income. This was no easy task as it required discipline for a twelve-year-old and a nineteen-year-old. Mrs. Van Wormer called me often. Usually her call related to some disciplinary problem with Gary. He was not a bad boy, he was just a big twelve-year-old with a sixty-year-old grandmother!

Mrs. Van Wormer and Lilly Bowen were the best of friends and spent a lot of time together. They had a lot in common in that they were both raising children who were not their own. Mrs. Van Wormer and Lilly's type of person are always important to any church, but in our case they were very important. Together, their families provided 50 percent of our membership, including the oldest and the youngest members.

Mrs. Van Wormer is now ninety years old and in poor health but still has her quick laugh. Dolly and Gary's mother is now living with her in the house where Mrs. Van Wormer has lived since she was married.

Her contribution as one of the original members would be difficult to measure because it was more in terms of consistency, stability in living, and attending than in measurable terms, such as bringing new members or financial giving.

Dolly Sherman Speaks About Her Grandmother, Dolly Van Wormer

My grandmother was born in 1894 in Buchanan, Virginia. She was the youngest of four children. She was raised by strict German parents, who made their living off the land. My grandmother was just becoming a young woman when her mother died. Her brothers left to go to the war [World War I]. Her sister married, leaving her to care for and work with her father, whom she feared because of his frequent displays of irrational temper.

During a visit to her married sister, my grandmother met the man she married. My grandfather was a devout Christian. He participated actively in his church and, I am sure, he headed a Christian household. They had two children, my mother and a son, William. My grandmother was quite young when my grandfather died.

When I was very young I knew my grandmother as an attractive, lighthearted, fun-loving lady. She always had an air of independence about her and displayed a strong character. She always seemed to be a highly moral, conscientious person. In her later years she began to show some of the behavioral traits that she had told us her father had displayed toward her. She seemed to be obsessed with what other people would think of her actions. However, she never seemed concerned about what we thought of ourselves.

I believed that in her own way she was deeply religious, though I feel she cheated herself out of much of the joy of her faith because of her staid convictions and by her preoccupation with trying to please other people instead of being pleased with herself.

She has always worked hard and much of her life has been spent in laboring at menial tasks of a domestic nature, although she always seemed proud of her position. She still displays the same strong-willed personality and pluck that we have known throughout much of her life.

She worked in the church and for the church and was always willing to help when she was able. She has always been willing to help others in need, despite the fact that she is rather an isolationist. People have most always spoken well of her, and she has never been without friends.

Disciple 7: Dolly Sherman

Dolly Sherman, from the very beginning, was one of our most active members. She was a good musician, a good softball player, and loved to talk. I had a personal interest in the same areas, so I enjoyed many interesting conversations with Dolly.

She invited a lot of people to the church, but her greatest contribution was through her music. She played the trumpet and sang exceptionally well. After high school, she worked for an insurance company but later earned her living by performing and teaching music. First-time visitors to our church were always surprised at the quality of the music. Few expected much from such a small gathering in such an unusual place. Dolly, along with other members who will be introduced later, was largely responsible for the music.

Her contribution to the church development was very evident. But I believe the contribution the church made to her life was equally as great. Since she lived with a grand-mother without a mother or father, her need for adult atten-tion and encouragement was greater than for most her age. She got encouragement in abundance from the people of the church. The fact that she was one of the original mem-bers made her feel confident in performing before the con-gregation. I feel this experience in the church also provided confidence necessary for performing in secular settings.

Dolly Sherman Speaks

I was born August 3, 1935 in Baltimore, Maryland. When I was four years old my mother and I moved to the old farm home in Fort Foote. I lived there with my grandmother and great uncle for twenty-eight years. During my early years, my family attended church sporadically.

My mother remarried and left the area when my brother was a few years old. My grandmother was faced with the responsibility of raising my brother and me at a very difficult period of her life and an equally difficult period in history, as America was in the midst of World War II. I can still remember the air raids, the blackouts, and the searchlights sweeping the sky at night. We were a lot more fortunate than some people because at least we had the land. My uncle had a good farm and several thousand chickens, so there was always something to eat. The chicken feed was delivered in brightly printed sacks which my grand-mother would work magic over and transform into crisp dresses and shorts and blouses for my brother and me.

Even though times were hard and we never had a great deal of material wealth, we never thought of ourselves as poor. We wouldn't dare to even think of being poor because my grandmother was a very proud and enterprising lady who encouraged, in fact, demanded us to be independent. We were also taught to be creative.

When I was nine years old I expressed a great love for the outdoors, so I took to the fields with my Uncle Jay.

Uncle Jay was a quiet man, and I loved being with him. He taught me many things about the ground and gave me a deep love for the earth and growing things. This closeness to the earth became an integral part of my life. Being so close to nature provided a tremendous opportunity to think and dream and plan for my future.

My grandmother was a very strict disciplinarian who always demanded the very best of me. While I was small, she could control my actions, but my teenage years brought a lot of conflicts both within myself and the family.

In high school, I was introduced to music. Then I didn't realized what a major part this was to play in my life's plans. During my remaining school years, music was to be my main source of identity among my peers.

In spite of my strong attraction to the creative arts, I continued to have a great deal of trouble in school. Many times I was bored and discontented and became a discipline problem both in school and at home. My last year of school I lived with my aunt and uncle. They were loving, warm people but were still very strict, though I did gain a certain amount of freedom. They insisted that I go to church, which I did reluctantly. I did manage to graduate from high school but certainly was not looked upon as one most likely to succeed.

I moved back to Fort Foote after high school. I continued to study music and played in some small civic groups. I passed up an opportunity to join the Women's Air Force Band. The thought of going to college was out of the question. Aside from not having the money, my family felt that a high school education was adequate preparation for a good job. After several short-term jobs, I finally went to work for an insurance company where I worked for fourteen years.

During this period I did continue to keep up with my music as best I could; but, I had pretty well given up on the idea of music as a profession. I fell into the typical apathetic rut. I worked and slept and socialized once in a while, and went to church whenever the spirit moved me, which wasn't too often at this point.

Then one day some young people came to visit us from Congress Heights Baptist Church. They wanted to build a church in our neighborhood. There were tent meetings and meetings in people's homes and then finally the first real church service in my Uncle Jay's little fruit stand. I am sure that the disciples had more space in the upper room than we had in that little fruit stand with a lectern and heating stove.

Well, they figured out how to get me out of bed on Sunday morning. They asked me if I could provide the music. Can you imagine a trumpet in such a small building? I don't know yet if it were self-preservation or a sympathetic pastor, but we really had close communion with a piano, a lectern, and twelve chairs all in a 10' x 20' building.

The church began to grow and pretty soon we had Sunday School classes in people's homes all over Fort Foote, including mine. There are so many wonderful memories of those humble beginnings.

Those meetings in that tiny building that I had helped my uncle build were to be the beginning of my life. I wasn't an easy convert. I still had a lot of years of conflict and rebellion to overcome. I still had dreams that needed to be realized and goals to fulfill. Though I had been baptized when I was eight or nine years old, I didn't become a born-again Christian until I was twenty-two. I thought I was being called to be a missionary, but I learned very quickly that I couldn't lead until I had learned to follow. I didn't become a missionary, but the Lord chose rather to reveal to me that I had a voice and once again I was drawn back to music.

There were many deep spiritual and emotional experiences in the humble beginnings of Fort Foote Church. The physical appearances of the buildings have changed from the tiny fruit stand to the beautiful brick church that now stands where fields of narcissus and daffodils once grew. But, the greatest changes were in the people's lives. The buildings will one day pass and decay, but the profound love and caring of Reverends Carrol Bruce and Charles Leonard will live forever in the lives that they touched through their ministries.

I haven't made any mountainous mark thus far in my life. I still feel that I have a lot of growing to do. I still feel that I am in the process of becoming whatever or whoever God wants me to be.

I am now nearly fifty years old, have had the privilege of attending college, and singing and playing in some of the largest and most presti- gious churches in the Washington area. I taught instrumental music for six years in the Catholic school system and had my own music program for four years on two military bases nearby, working with children of military personnel.

I have recently retired with a dear friend on a small farm in upper Montgomery County where I enjoy gardening and working with our four show horses. I still enjoy my music and still do some free-lance teaching.

I feel so richly blessed by being able to realize so many of my dreams and aspirations. Above all, I am more and more aware every day of God's infinite capacity to love us, no matter how difficult we are to love, and of his miracle of love and grace that overtook my life back in that crowded little fruit stand so many years ago.

Disciple 8: Gary Sherman

Gary probably did more for the church in its earlier days than he ever realized. He helped me to relate to boys his age long before I had a son of my own. I've mentioned before that Mrs. Van Wormer called me often about discipline problems with him because he had a way, as most twelve-year-old boys do, of taking her to the limit. This meant wearing out her patience or taking her to the point of not knowing what to do with him. At those times, she would talk to me about him.

On one occasion she called and I went to talk to Gary. He used the same approach to me he had with Mrs. Van Wormer, which was open defiance. I said to him, "Since you don't have a father, I am going to pretend that I am your father and do what he, or at least some fathers, would do." So, I proceeded to cut a long switch off a nearby tree and put teeth in my threat with a couple of surprise lashes on his back. They were light, but shocking. Amazingly enough, our relationship got better rather than worse.

Gary was such a friendly boy that everyone liked him almost as much as I did. His contribution was that he helped us all to understand the reality of a boy's world. This reality was a big factor in the church's keeping in touch with young people. He is now married, has two teenage children, and lives in Roanoke, Virginia.

When he was moving to Roanoke a few years ago to take a new job, he and his family stopped by to see us in Charlottesville, Virginia. I felt very proud of the part our church had in the development of his life and grateful for the role he played as one of the original twelve members.

Disciple 9: Sara Redman

Sara Redman was in her late thirties, the mother of four children, and working as a bank teller for the Anacostia Bank in D.C. Her oldest and youngest daughters had attended the prayer and Bible study meetings at the Dalton's house, which was just across the street from where the Redmans lived. However, neither Sara nor her husband Dave had attended. Sara was a good pianist. In addition to her job as a bank teller, she earned extra money by occasionally playing the piano at a restaurant on Indian Head Highway not far from where our church was meeting. Sara had not been active in church for several years, though she was a member of a Baptist church in North Carolina.

My first direct contact with her was a call from Georgetown University Hospital. She was there with her husband who had cut his shoulder in a near-tragic accident. Twenty-nine stitches closed the cut, but a blood clot had formed, threatening his life. Sara knew of me because her daughters attended the meetings in the Dalton home. When she felt the need for a minister, she called me. I went immediately to the hospital and talked with her. Dave survived the blood clot crisis, but it was some time before he had full use of his arm.

The following Sunday Sara came to our church and publicly rededicated her life. She began playing the piano for us rather than at the restaurant.

She was a very energetic person, capable of holding two jobs. When Dave was unable to work, she supported the family with an equal amount of determination, will, and ability. As one of the original twelve members, she gave as much leadership as anyone else in the early days of the church. She and her family were with us for about two years before they moved to North Carolina. She teamed with Dolly Sherman and Bill Richards, who was to become our first music director, to provide the music for our services.

Sara had been away from the church for several years. According to her own testimony, she had lived accordingly. When she came back, I am sure she was more zealous and loyal to the church than ever before. She believed in and supported our church to the extreme extent that on one occasion she refused to give money to charity through the bank, choosing to give all she could afford to the church.

At her work and in her life, she was a good example of what the church could do for an individual. This was demonstrated when it came time for us to borrow money to build a permanent church building from the bank where she worked. She also led her husband and children to make commitments to Christ. They were all baptized into the church.

Sara Redman Speaks

I was christened, raised, and at the age of ten sprinkled in a church in my hometown in North Carolina. At the age of twelve, after having studied music since I was six old, I became pianist of the church and was very active in all aspects of the Methodist church until I married at age nineteen and moved to another city. All of my life I wanted to be a good "born again," "baptized," "immersed" in water, saved by faith and God's grace, and go to heaven when I died. I also wanted to play the piano for the Lord! I walked sawdust trails at tent meetings, any time, any church. I walked the aisle at altar calls looking for that satisfied, wonderful feeling of God's simple plan of salvation that I was longing for but ignorant of how, why, and where to accept Christ.

At age twenty-one, my husband was killed in an automobile crash, leaving me with a mentally retarded daughter and a two weeks old baby. My Christian uncle and aunt took us into their home to live.

It was at the Glenhope Baptist Church that I found Christ as my personal Savior. Now I had what I had been looking for all of my childhood and teenage life!

With a group of eight to ten Christians from Glenhope church, we went every week to home prayer meetings. I played an accordion as accompaniment for a duet and quartet. Our mission was to teach and show sinners how to be saved and accept Christ's love. We finally found a "store house" to hold meetings in, and one of the members studying for the ministry, Reverend Eugene Hancock, our pastor, helped to build, with God's help and faithful Christians, Andrews Memorial Baptist Church in North Carolina where he was pastor until his untimely death a few years ago. One of our singers was a fourteen-year-old teenager from Glenhope Baptist Church, whom I had the privilege of teaching to play the accordion. She has been a minister of music and still plays the accordion and has sung at Andrews Memorial Baptist Church for forty years. I have an LP recording of the choir and music—beautiful!

Time passes and circumstances alter your life, your work, and your going to school for higher education. I moved with my family to the Washington, D.C., area to be near my mother and my sister, thus meeting and marrying the man who is my husband today. We lived in Fort Foote Village. The nearest church was a Methodist church in Oxon Hill, Maryland. We did visit there but I had left my membership at a Baptist church in North Carolina.

My daughter, who was a junior in high school, was attending a weekly prayer meeting across the street from our home led by Carrol Bruce and his wife Frances, from Congress Heights Baptist Church. My daughter would tell me about the wonderful prayer meeting and ask me to go. But at this time I had strayed from the Good Shepherd's fold—away from my church, working for Jesus, and was utterly miserable! The prayer meeting moved to a fruit stand (owned by Mr. Green, but at that time he had not accepted Christ as his personal Savior).

A near tragedy in my life brought me back to my knees. With God's help, prayers from friends, loved ones, "Preacher Bruce," and his wife Frances, I came to the fruit stand where twelve of us Christians dedicated ourselves to working for Christ.

Yes! We had a piano and I played it. God blessed us so abundantly. We were poor in monetary ways but rich in the blessings of Christ. We all tithed. We had a real purpose in mind, building a church in a much-needed community. Sin was rampant.

We outgrew our fruit stand so Mr. Green let us use his feed barn. A memorable time (and there were so many) was getting our new building (feed barn). Our goal was to hold our first Easter service there. We did and had seventy-five in attendance. What a beautiful, joyful, happy time in the Lord! He was really showing us the fruit of serving, worshiping, giving, teaching, and, most of all, letting our lives be a living testimony for Christ. He can save a sinner and reclaim a backslider and give us eternal life with a joy down in our hearts that only the born-again child of God can know.

Then we had a revival. Yes! Our "Preacher Bruce" was the preacher. Mr. Green had already made his public acceptance. I was playing the piano. On the invitation, my husband and my teenage son came forward and accepted Christ as their personal Savior. More answered prayers, more joy and happiness beyond comprehension. Our dear Heavenly Father had really worked miracles saving the lost, bringing in new members. Our church did so much for our community too. Then we had our first baptismal service at Congress Heights Baptist Church one Sunday afternoon. Mr. Green, my husband, Dave, and my son Bobby, were baptized. Words cannot express the joy I felt on that occasion.

There stands today built by God, faith, prayer, and on a firm foundation a big, brick, beautiful house of the Lord—Fort Foote Baptist Church. Some of the early members have gone to be with the Lord. Some are living in different states, serving in their respective churches. My own family—children and grandchildren—are "born-again Christians."

They serve as teachers, pastors, and singers. God blessed us with musical talent, and it is being used for his glory. I am including my sister, her family, cousins, and friends. We keep in touch as much as possible and visit the Fort Foote Baptist Church when we go to Maryland. Thank God for his Son who died on the cross to save a sinner like me and give us eternal life.

Disciple 10: Maudice Roberts

Maudice Roberts was a registered nurse in her forties and worked for the government in a supervisory capacity. She had been married to Odell Roberts for several years. They had no children. Maudice told me that she was a member of a church in North Carolina and had not attended anywhere regularly since she was in nurses' training. Her husband had never been a member of any church and was not a professing Christian at that time. They owned a home in the community and had lived there for several years. Mr. Roberts died about two years ago, and Mrs. Roberts lives in that same house and is presently the clerk of the Fort Foote Baptist Church.

Mrs. Roberts started attending the church services about the same time as Sara Redman. Their husbands were acquaintances. Sara and Maudice probably met each other through their husbands. They had much in common. They were both from North Carolina and both had a lot of determination, will, and ability. Mrs. Roberts was a tower of strength in the early days of the church and remains so to this day.

A special contribution of hers to the church in the beginning days was her ability to relate to all kinds of people. In her mind, no one was better or worse, higher or lower than she was. She related to all who came in the same way and could convey to others that feeling. Also, she added a certain business touch to our group. She saw endeavors of the church as good business or bad business. This may seem unimportant to spiritual development, but unless that dimension is there, something very important is missing and the development of the church is slower. Unless really "providentially hindered," she was present at every meeting—running a little late but always there.

Mr. Roberts did not attend church very often. But he and I became good friends through Mrs. Roberts. From where we lived, we went by their house almost every day and would often stop and chat if they were out in the yard. Later, when I was away at the seminary, they showed a special interest in Frances and the children which, of course, strengthened my appreciation for them. Mrs. Roberts, more than any of the original twelve members, has kept in contact with us over the years and is the only one of the original twelve who is presently in attendance at Fort Foote Baptist Church.

Disciple 11: Frances Bruce

Frances and I are the other two of the original twelve. Everything we did was a sharing endeavor. Sometimes I was the one out front, but more often than might be expected she was. The best example of that is when I was away at the seminary. For three years of this six-year involvement with the church, I was away at Southeastern Baptist Theological Seminary in Wake Forest, North Carolina. For two of the other years I was on active duty with the Air Force. Frances was more than a pastor's wife during these six years. In her low-key way, she did very effective pastoring with the people. This was in addition to being the mother of two small children. Robert was born in 1956 just a little over one year after the beginning of the church.

I have often said in talking about the first twelve members that I was a frustrated Air Force officer and none of the other members had a normal church relationship at the time of

our beginning, except Frances. In truth, from the beginning, she was the most stabilizing force in the church. She
did her part and made sure my part was done too.

Frances Bruce Speaks

My father was thirty-five years older than my mother. After seventeen
years of marriage and six children, my mother left my father. My mother
took the youngest child with her, but left my dad with the other five,
including me. I was ten years old. One by one, the three older children
and one younger left home to live with other families who offered them
a home in return for their help with farm work. By doing this they were
able to finish high school.

My younger brother and I were the only children left with Dad when
my six-year-old sister, who had been living with Mom, returned to live
with us. After my mom left, I saw my dad's health deteriorate to the
point where he was never himself again and unable to care for us. He
had been a good, honest, moral man all his life. I wanted so badly to
be of help to him in these last years of his life. When he died, I was
almost fifteen years old and my sister was eleven.

We had no place to live so Clifford and Ada Tanner took us to live
with them. They did not know us but had known my dad from the
fur-trapping business. They helped my sister Pauline and me get into a
private Christian girls school named Kentucky Female Orphans' School.
It was there that I learned about Christ and the Christian way of life. At
sixteen, I committed my life to Jesus Christ. After I accepted Christ as
Savior, I had a lot of changes to make. I felt a strong commitment to
the Tanner family. They meant so much to me, and I wanted to do well
in school and make them proud of me.

At that point I again made contact with my mom. Instead of express-
ing bitterness toward her for leaving my dad, I expressed reconciliation.
This enabled me to go on with life without a burden of guilt.

After graduation from junior college, I went to work for the University
of Kentucky. There I met my future husband, Carrol Bruce.

Carrol was a deeply religious person, and I had already decided I
would not seriously date anyone who was not a Christian. Still, deciding

to marry him was a difficult decision. In my mind, I was committed to a lifetime marriage, and I didn't want my children to go through what I had gone through with my mom and dad's marriage. Within two years, we were married.

When Carrol discussed his feeling that God wanted him in full-time church work as a pastor and wanted to know how I felt about it, I really didn't know what to say. I just felt that I had to examine my life and more or less say, "Here I am, just as I am, help me to become the person you would have me to be." As I look back on that time, I think I was a very important person in Carrol's life, and I felt a definite calling to be a minister's wife.

About a year and a half after going to Washington, D.C., we moved out into the countryside of Fort Foote, Maryland, where the church was. Carrol was still in the Air Force, and everything was easy. When his time with the Air Force was over, we decided to stay in the same house while Carrol commuted to Southeastern Seminary in Wake Forest, North Carolina. Life became very different, very quickly. Carrol left for the seminary on Monday and returned on Friday. This lasted three years and caused me a lot of problems. I wanted to go to the seminary, too, and thought I needed it more than Carrol. He grew up in a Christian home and had a good background in Christianity. I was the one who really needed to be exposed to Christian teachings at the seminary. But, financially, we could not both go to seminary. So I stayed in the Fort Foote area and cared for the church people and our two children.

I made the best of what I thought was a bad situation. As it turned out, it was a time of development for me as a person. I did not plan it that way but just lived and related to the church members naturally, listening and caring daily. I never had a game plan, nor did I organize any type of visitation or caring program. As needs arose and opportunities came, our two children and I went and helped. Sometimes it was just listening to someone over the telephone. Usually I didn't need to have a set answer for them. I just listened unhurriedly. I learned to stand on my own two feet. I learned to go to God more for help, and our relationship grew along with my relationship to the church members until they became my enlarged family.

Growing up without my mother in the home helped me to immediately understand the pains of the original twelve. They trusted my Christian response to their problems because I had walked where they had walked.

Disciple 12: Carrol Bruce

I was third in a family of seven children. This made me almost six years younger than my sister and almost four years younger than my brother, Herbert, Jr. Since ours was a farm family, capacity to work was of high value to my parents.

On the farm, there was just one way for me to get equal recognition with my brother. I had to do more work than was expected of me. Even now, I have a strong memory of telling myself at the beginning of the day, "Plant five more rows, hoe five more rows, or plow five more rows than they expect." Or, more often, I would decide to do the amount of work expected of Herb, Jr., which would take working a little faster or a little longer.

The work was hard, but I loved every day of it and thought that I would always want to be a farmer. There was much goal setting, complete freedom to work on goals, and great satisfaction when I reached them. Our kind of farming put me against the opposition, which was the work to be done. I really enjoyed that kind of challenge. I learned when I was willing to discount the odds, work a little harder, try different ways of doing things, set a specific goal and commit myself to reaching it, I could usually do what needed to be done.

Commitment was a word used around the church more than in our home. My parents believed as much in the local church as they did in work. They demonstrated their belief by their loyalty to the church. My dad, who is now eighty years old, has been a member of the Mount Pisgah Baptist Church since he was about twelve years old. My mother joined that church when they were married more than sixty years ago. Just to indicate how loyal they have been, they were very reluctant to come to hear me when I first started preaching because they didn't want to miss the service in their own church. They were not only loyal in attendance but also believed in what the church stood for as verbalized by the preacher. This included a considerable scope of virtues with the top one being honesty. My parents are probably the most honest people I know. For them, to make a promise is to keep it.

When our family commits itself to do something we have to do it. The odds against it, adverse circumstances, lack of resources, or whatever, are considered before the commitment is made. But once made, it must be kept. I learned from my parents that one never asked whether one would keep a commitment or not, but simply how one would keep it.

I remember my early college days, which certainly marked the beginning of a new life for me. Herb, Jr., had been working during the two years after his graduation. He and I enrolled in the University of Kentucky together. Since he had worked for two years, he had more money than I had, but not a lot more. I had three hundred dollars which I had earned the summer after graduation from high school.

There were many times when quitting or dropping out for a while to work was tempting, but I can very honestly say that I never seriously considered it. With encouragement from my parents, former teachers, and friends, who seemed to believe in me, I always found a way to earn enough money to stay in school.

Amazingly enough, what seemed to be only hard work to most people was really fun for me. The challenge was great and the opposition strong, but the joy and satisfaction in accomplishing my purpose was so rewarding that life seemed more good than bad. These family concepts uniquely prepared me to stick with the original twelve until we truly became a church.

4

The Move to a Feed Storage Building

Mr. Green attended all the services that we held in his building, except the first one. By the time we outgrew the first building, he had become very interested in what we were doing. After our "worship-standing-up" experience, I approached him about the use of the larger feed storage building. This time he was very willing for us to use it, but he still needed it for storage. This building was right on the main road. It would seat at least 125 people and could easily be made to look like a church. I suggested we build a smaller building for storage near his chicken houses so we could have the one near the road. He agreed, and our new project took a giant step forward.

Some of us dug the footing. Bucky Dalton's brother-in-law, Wayne Sisson, laid the block; we all put on the roof. When this little building was finished, just about our entire congregation, which was not much more than thirty-five, began to clean and renovate the feed building. We cleaned out about two feet of accumulated feed and debris, put in a new ceiling, painted the walls inside and out, repaired the roof, and made two little rooms for a nursery just inside the front door. We moved our piano from the previous building, bought more folding chairs, and installed a fairly new space heater given by one of the new families. We were really in the church development business in a great way. A convert- ed feed house doesn't seem adequate for a worship place, but it was a lot better than a converted roadside fruit and vegetable stand!

There was one other major job that had to be done before we could conveniently use the new facility. The trees and thicket that had grown up around it had to be cut and moved away. Coming from a farm, I had more expertise in doing this kind of work than most of the others. With the help of Harold Hodges, who was a member of Congress Heights Baptist Church and an airman in my Air Force office, we soon cleared a large parking space around the building. Our church, with the name over the front door, could now be seen by everyone who traveled the Fort Foote Road. The day we held our first service in the new building was a proud moment.

We still owned no land or property. But to know Mr. Green was to know that when he said that we could use the building he meant that we could use it until his death.

Mr. Green retired from the chicken business. He had plenty of time to visit with me, which we did at every opportunity. He loved to tell about his experiences in the cavalry in World War I, and I enjoyed hearing them. He never missed a church service. During the first year in the new building, he made a public profession of faith in Christ and was baptized into our fellowship. From that point on, the church was really his life.

One of the reasons we built the little nursery rooms in our new building was that Anna was now two years old and our second child was expected later that year. Rob was born in December and joined the babies of other young families who had started attending.

Having this greatly improved building gave us a boost in morale, strengthened our pride, and inspired us to work even harder to get more people involved in our church. The Fort Foote community was beginning to grow in population which gave us more new prospects. Between our church and the Potomac River, the land was being subdivided for houses and sold at a price of five thousand dollars per half acre, which was rather expensive at that time. The people who bought into the area were those who had a higher than average income, certainly, much higher than the average longtime residents of the area. We had to begin thinking about how to reach out and include these new people.

To do this, we simply continued our efforts to invite friends, respond to needs that the church knew about, and make as many other direct contacts as we had opportunity. As the population grew, more and more people had to drive by our church every day on their way to work. If they attended a church in D.C., they drove by again on Sunday. Some of them began to stop to worship with us, rather than drive into town. We were beginning to be seen as a real church by others than the non-Christians, inactive church members, or people in crisis. Of our first seventy-five official members, about fifty were baptized into our fellowship. This began to change and more people were joining by transfer of membership from other churches. Ours was the only church of any denomination in the community.

We expanded our services to include a mid-week prayer service and had special meetings, such as revivals, like the more established churches. We still had few officers and no organization except Sunday School. Our philosophy was that we would let the need dictate the offices and organizations rather than the reverse. It was not until we moved into our permanent building two years later that we selected our first deacons.

I mentioned before that our sponsoring church had not provided personnel, but two individuals did come from that congregation at my request to help with music. Both were key people in the development of the church. Bill Richards was a nineteen-year-old airman from Texas. He was a nice-looking young man with a very friendly personality. He loved to sing but had little opportunity to do so at the mother church because it was a large church with many people who did "special" singing. I heard about Bill through mutual friends and asked him to help us. Our situation seemed just right for a young man who planned to do church music, and he wholeheartedly accepted. He led our singing, sang solos, and enlisted others to do "special" singing. In a very real sense, he was our music director.

Under his leadership our music program attracted many new people. Probably more important, Bill grew as a person. He married his Texas girlfriend and stayed with us the two remaining years of his Air Force enlistment. Until the latter part of the time Bill was with us, we didn't have an organized choir. He had an unusual ability for a person his age to involve all the congregation in singing in a way that made each person feel like a choir member participating in the most important worship service of one's life.

When we were meeting in the roadside stand, Mrs. Snead brought her son, Herman, and his friend Mabel with her. I suspect bringing these two was the motivating reason for her coming. I don't know Mabel's background except that she was a very fine person with a previous rocky marriage and a very lovely daughter.

Herman was different. He was in his late thirties, had lived a very hard life up to that point, and was divorced. The kind of life he lived did not make for any kind of marriage. Herman had never been a member of any church. To my knowledge, with the exception of Mabel, his close friends were little help to him in living a better life. I visited a friend of his in the hospital once. While Herman was there visiting, they both excused themselves to take a drink that Herman had brought to the patient. The patient got out of bed at some risk to his life to go down the hall with Herman to take the drink so I wouldn't see them.

Even though he was anything but a churchman, with encouragement from his mother and Mabel, he continued to attend. In spite of the life he was living, he was a very capable cook and manager of a food counter not far from our church. He was able to hold his job in spite of being off from work more than normal. He lived with his mother on Rhode Island Avenue, about an hour's drive from the church, and continued to come to our services. At first, I believe he came just to satisfy his mother and Mabel. I remember at one of the services, after he had been coming for several months, he took communion. Mrs. Snead didn't know what that meant regarding his relationship to God, but she remarked to me how thrilled she was about it.

As his interest grew, Herman asked for a visit from me. I visited with him about every two weeks in their apartment to discuss questions he had about becoming a Christian and living the Christian life. After about six months, he made a public profession of faith in Christ and presented himself for baptism into our church. Several others had done this in our meetings before, but none seemed to affect the congregation more than Herman. One day I counted thirteen adults in our worship service whom Herman had invited. They were people who worked for him, as well as friends from his previous life. Being a friendly and capable man, he began to do even better in his work. Not long after becoming an active member of the church, he got a job as a salesman for a food company and was even more successful. He became an usher as soon as one was needed and was an active deacon at the time of his death in the late sixties.

One of my most gratifying rewards from the Fort Foote experience was the annual letter that Herman sent us from the time we left the church until his death. It was never a long letter but expressed simply his appreciation for church and our interest in him.

Our first big event in the feed building church was Herman and Mabel's wedding. The guests were members of our congregation who had become their closest friends. For this occasion we removed the pulpit, which was between the space heater and the piano, to make that area the marriage altar. After Bill Richards sang, Herman and Mabel came out of the nursery rooms and walked down the aisle between the folding chairs. I thought it was one of the most beautiful wedding processions that I had ever seen.

The church continued to grow. One Sunday morning, when we arrived for worship, parked next to the church was a cream-colored Cadillac that looked almost as long as the building. The owner of this automobile was the commanding officer of the Anacostia Naval Air Station. He had bought a new home overlooking the Potomac River near our church. His was a very devout Christian family. Rather than look elsewhere for a place to worship they had come to our church. They were a delightful family and brought with them a broader understanding of the Christian life than many of our new Christians had. One rainy day when I was going into D.C. I passed the wife of this commanding officer helping an elderly man of the community into her car. He was known to be mentally ill. Sometimes he would escape from home and walk up and down the road, even in the rain. She put him in her car and drove him home.

Our feed storage church building was much appreciated and cared for. It provided adequate space for our worship service but not for Sunday School. We had curtained off rooms for four classes. That was not enough to have a separate class for each age group of our congregation. Since there wasn't any more space, we did the only thing that was left to do. We asked for a home for the Junior, Intermediate, and Young People's departments as they were known at that time. The Williams, Mers, and Bruce families provided the homes for these departments. Some of the teachers were from these homes and provided the necessary transportation from the Sunday School class in the home to the worship service in the church. All that the parents had to do was to drop their children off at the proper place for Sunday School. This arrangement continued until we began meeting in our permanent building. This system worked so well that I used it later in two other places with equal or greater success where Sunday School space in the church building was not available.

Now additions were largely new people in the community, but we continued to get crisis people from bordering communities. Word got around that our people could identify with almost any type of crisis. This gave us a larger ministry than most churches our size and certainly more than we were prepared for or trained to handle. I learned very early that helping some people was far beyond the scope of my own resources. Friendship and love did help, regardless of the problem.

There was nothing unusual about our worship services, except that we sat closer together because of crowded conditions. We did have good music for the size of our congregation. The visitors usually remarked about the gladness and joy in our members more than anything else. This positive feeling must have come from a sense of accomplishment on their part. Many of them had started coming to church out of a crisis situation and had received life-changing help. This "glad-I-am-here" feeling was contagious. And, as in any church, the intangibles are usually more significant than what is seen or touched. Physical closeness affected our worship. On occasion, I had just enough room to stand to preach. With my limited training and experience, I didn't know very much about how to preach anyway. I worked hard at trying. Once I looked back over my notes from that time. I decided the people who listened to me must have been the most gracious and needy who ever attended a worship service. I felt the sermons were so bad that I threw them away and tried not to remember them.

The Move to a Feed Storage Building

After we moved into our feed building church, we still had problems. Our heating stove, which burned fuel oil, gave off a constant odor. This was offensive to some, and others thought it might be dangerous. It was very hot near the stove but rather cold farther away. The front-row people looked like it was summertime while back-row people looked like it was winter.

Another problem was that the front entrance was very close to the main highway, which made traffic annoying and distracting during the service. It was also dangerous as people entered and left the building. We had signs put up at both approaches to our property, but that still did not slow some who often appeared to be trying to create a problem.

At one of our evening services, several dogs began barking and fighting right next to the building. We thought they would stop or go away, but, after what seemed like forever, they were still barking. I stopped preaching while Kenny Bowen and a couple of his friends ran the dogs away.

In spite of these and other occasional problems, we had many good times together in our feed building church.

5
Community Relations and Influence

One of my duties in the Air Force was to attend monthly training sessions for special agents. The program was usually presented by the head of an investigative organization other than the O.S.I. One of the first I attended was conducted by the chief of the Washington Metropolitan Police Department.

At the beginning of his lecture, he placed a map of the greater Washington area on the wall and pointed out that the Fort Foote area was the place where more sex-related crimes were committed than any in other Washington area. To prove it, he cited two rather recent homicide cases. Fort Foote was one of the few undeveloped areas close to the District of Columbia. This made it an attractive place for criminal activity.

Upon hearing this statement from the Metropolitan Police chief, my special agent friend who knew we were in the process of developing a church there glanced at me to see my reaction. I was surprised and shocked but challenged even more by the need for a church in a community like that.

From the beginning there were people in the community who really wanted to see a church there, as well as those who thought one could not succeed. The man responsible for the small housing development on Fort Foote Terrace had suggested to the Congress Heights Baptist Church earlier, and to me later, that he would like to help get one started. His idea was to build one building for both a community recreational center and a church. He felt that having such a facility would encourage new people to move into the area. It sounded good to me, except that he would provide the land only if such a facility was always under his control. I never knew what he meant by being under his control, but my experience with Baptist churches was that they were never controlled by anyone except the membership. Obviously, this arrangment would not work. We did explore the possibility for some time, but the owner was never willing to provide land for a building to be under total control of the church.

After the church had been established, it did begin to influence new people to move into the community. Realtors told me prospective land and home buyers always asked about school and very often about church facilities in the area. The man who owned and operated the garage often gave a rather large financial donation, even though neither he nor any member of his family attended. Periodically, when I stopped to buy gas or to have my car serviced, he would give me a check for the church and say that he felt it was helpful to the community. Years later more than one member of his family did join the church and became active in it.

Quite often after Herman and Mabel were married, unchurched people would ask me to perform their wedding ceremonies. Their coming to me indicated that we had achieved some "church status" in the community.

During my six years as pastor of the Fort Foote Church, there was only one death among our approximately three hundred members. Ray and Peggy Long's son, Mark, died when he was only two years old. There were several other deaths in the community, and I was asked to conduct many of the funeral services. Usually, when new people moved into the community, a brief welcome-to-the-community-contact was made by me or a member of the congregation. This kind of contact apparently was sufficient to establish the presence of our church in their minds. When a death or a serious illness occurred, I was often contacted.

I think it should be noted here that community in and around Washington, D.C., at that time was much more significant and respected than it is now. Community boundary lines were much more definable then than now, and this was especially true in our area. The District of Columbia border line was on one side, Indian Head Highway on another, and the Potomac River on another. The other side was open-ended, but the new community of Fort Washington was growing in that direction and provided something of a boundary between us. These boundaries gave us a natural geographic community, which was very significant in the development of our church.

As recognition and respect for our church began to increase, amazingly enough it seemed to carry into the Air Force. In the beginning, my immediate supervisors were not sure they wanted an ordained minster in their organization. By the time we we were meeting in the feed building, this attitude had changed noticeably.

The President, by executive order, required attendance at lectures on how to defend against brainwashing. More than in the previous wars, this was a real problem in the Korean War. Much publicity had been given to P.O.W.s' brainwashing.

My immediate superior officer was in charge of this training program and asked me to give a lecture on the "Belief in God as a Defense Against Brainwashing." All 250 people of the O.S.I. organization at Bolling Field attended the lecture. At that time that was the largest gathering I had spoken to, and I was really scared. I do not know how much the speech helped brainwashing prevention, but it did help me and my church. From that point on, I was never asked to serve as Saturday night or Sunday duty officer. The schedule was prepared so that I had only weekday duty for the remainder of my tour with the Air Force.

At that training session, I was introduced as an ordained Baptist minister who was involved in starting a church at Fort Foote. Most of the people in the organization knew neither of these facts. In addition to affecting the duty roster, the revelation of these facts decreased considerably the number of invitations I received to attend parties given by O.S.I. personnel.

Maybe the most important reason our church was able to relate to the community was the simple kind of worship service we had. If our facilities had been sufficient, we would, no doubt, have had a more elaborate service and other programs that I had grown up with in Kentucky. Since we did not have space for those, we stayed with the basics. The average worshiper was happy with music, Scripture, and a sermon. Many other activities in the worship may be enjoyable, but congregational participation and the proclamation of the gospel were enough. When people get involved with a sermon, they feel that they have been to church.

The limited facilities, our background, and our limited experience were often translated into humility in the minds of our visitors and members. What would appear to be a disadvantage actually worked to our advantage in getting established in the community.

6
Out of Space Again

By the middle of 1957, we were beginning to need more space. We were not standing throughout the worship services as we once did in the fruit stand, but there were often no empty seats. Three Sunday School departments were being held in three homes. Mr. Green had no more buildings to lend us. We still owned no land and had no prospect of owning any in the near future. Our per capita offerings were good but were little more than enough to meet operational expenses.

In our minds, we knew something would have to be done to give us growing room, but we just didn't know what it would be. As I reflect back on our situation at that time, I think we probably didn't know enough about the normal procedure for church development to be discouraged. We continued to live one week at a time. Every Sunday was a refreshing change from our week's living and working and gave us strength for the new week. More than any group that I have known, with the possible exception of some small Christian groups in Japan, we looked forward to being together on Sunday.

In June 1957, I finished my tour of duty with the Air Force and was ready for seminary. Having grown up in Kentucky, I had always planned to attend The Southern Baptist Theological Seminary in Louisville, which was about 150 miles from my home and the East Union Church where I was first called to pastor. Even after coming to the Washington area with the Air Force, I thought I would go back there to attend seminary.

Life for Frances and me had greatly changed during the two years in the Air Force. The Fort Foote church was the major change. Seminary was a must for me. Frances wanted to attend also, but we just couldn't leave the church. We thought there must be some way to stay with the church and attend seminary at the same time. However, the closest Southern Baptist seminary to Washington was in Wake Forest, North Carolina, which is 260 miles away. Students often commute from church field to seminary but usually not quite that far. For us, though, there were really no other options. So, I enrolled in Southeastern Baptist Theological Seminary at Wake Forest.

The summer of 1957 was the first time I had been able to work full time for the church. That lasted only two months, as I enrolled in the seminary in September. While in the Air Force, I was always in the community to visit in the evenings, but now I would be away five days every week and could return only for emergencies. I would be leaving at noon on Monday and returning late Friday evening. The Air Force had occupied my time during the day but rarely after work. Seminary was different. For a person of my academic ability, it was very full time. The study load and a round trip of 520 miles seemed impossible. There was no I-95 at that time. It was a hard twelve-hour round trip.

As in most things that seem all bad, there is some good. This was true for me in the weekly trip to the seminary. When I first planned to attend Southeastern, someone told me that Bill Davenport in Alexandria, Virginia, had been commuting for a year to Southeastern. At that time, there was no Woodrow Wilson Bridge to join Alexandria and Fort Foote. So, we had to go through southeast Washington to get to Bill and Jean Davenport's house. The good that came from having to make this trip was that we got to know Bill and Jean Davenport. There were others who joined our car pool in Fredericksburg, but Bill was the one who was to influence me the most. With the exception of Frances and my parents, I believe Bill had more influence on my life and pastoral ministry than any other person.

During those long rides to the seminary, I learned a lot about pastoring from Bill. He was involved in starting a church, as I was. His understanding of the Christian life, his philosophy, and theology of the church were very different from mine. At first, I liked him, but I didn't accept his philosophy of the church. I did not agree with his understanding of the Christian life nor his theology. Thanks to his acceptance of me, I began to be more teachable in the seminary and more open to others, as he was with me. The kind of pastor I am now I owe to the time spent with Bill Davenport, commuting to the seminary. He became very much a part of the Fort Foote church development.

Seminary days were hard for me, but they were even harder for Frances. Being the mother of two small children, having a large responsibility with a young growing church, and living alone five days each week were difficult. Due to her ministry, the church never slowed in progress. As a result of that three-year experience, she became a lifetime copastor with me.

One week I drove our car to Fredericksburg, parked it on a side street, and rode from there to Wake Forest with another member of our car pool. During the week, someone crashed into the back of it, knocking it into a telephone pole. It looked like an accordion. The police finally traced the owner and came to our door at 2:00 AM. Frances says her heart stopped when she saw him, fearing that something had happened to me. From this episode, she discovered she could deal with emergencies as they came.

The main problem for most seminary students is money. I had gone on active duty just six months after the declared

national emergency was lifted, which meant there were no
G.I. benefits for military personnel whose terms of service
began after that time. We had not received a salary from the
church but lived solely off our Air Force income, which was
very adequate. Now it was different.

With the Air Force income gone and money for more than
just living expenses needed, the church needed to start paying a salary. This did not have to be suggested. A business
meeting was called to discuss what they should do and the
only question asked me was, "How much do you need for
living and seminary expenses?" The group had demonstrated many times that they could and would rise to cope with
difficult situations and meet unusual needs. Frances and I
determined how much we would need, and that was the
amount they gave us during our seminary years. When I
finished seminary, we had no debts and had lived very com-
fortably.

But I had encountered another very difficult problem
from the beginning of seminary that plagued me most of my
first year. Even though I had been exposed to formal education most of my life, I simply was not teachable in the seminary. I wanted a degree from a seminary, but I didn't want
any real changes in my life and ministry. This left me with
something less than a positive attitude toward those who
were trying to teach me, as well as toward the seminary in
general.

The most direct result of this attitude was that I was making low grades, especially in New Testament class. In my
second semester after a low grade on an important test, my
New Testament professor called me to his office. In brief, he
said, "I know the background of your type and your present
church and family situation, so I want to give you some
helpful advice. I think you can handle what I am going to
say. You have a good academic background, experience as
an officer in the Air Force, and in starting a church, as well

as being a family man. My advice is that you ought to either get with it, or get out." He said further that he saw it as very unethical for me to expose my wife to the hardships that she obviously was experiencing while I was away at seminary if I was determined not to learn anything while I was there. In saying all these things, his voice never faltered nor did his eyes look anywhere but toward me. I didn't like what I heard but left his office knowing full well that he was right and that I was wrong in the way I was approaching seminary education.

As a result of that meeting, I made a commitment to myself that I would at least attend every class with an open mind. Seminary life for me became more meaningful. Previous graduations had been matter of fact, but graduation from the seminary was tearful. My life had been opened in a way that directly influenced the growth of Fort Foote church.

The church was progressing in many different ways, and I believe a major factor in the progress was my being away most of the time attending seminary. Frances was giving a new dimension to pastoring that was coming solely from who she was as a person and how she related to the people. Also, the people were learning to depend more on themselves and less on me. They found that they could do a lot of what I had been doing. I confess that I thought my being away so much was bound to hinder the progress of the church. But I soon learned the meaning of the Scripture which says, "For I say . . . to every man . . . not to think of himself more highly than he ought to think" (Rom. 12:3).

7

Our Own Land

The church was making progress, but we still had no land of our own. The buildings that Mr. Green had made available to us were used as if they were our own. There never was any interference from him in what we did in remodeling, restructuring, or even clearing the land. He always acted as if he had actually given us the buildings and the surrounding land that we used for parking. In late 1957, the most unexpected transaction of the entire experience occurred.

I was at the church one day when I saw Mr. Green approaching. There was certainly nothing unusual about this because he visited quite often when I was there. We had become good friends and both enjoyed conversation that related to my farm experiences and his war experiences. This day the conversation was different.

He said, "I have heard you say many times that before we could have the most effective church, we would have to have land for a permanent church building. So, I have decided to give you some land."

He said this in a very matter-of-fact way, and I tried to respond accordingly. I said, "How much do you plan to give us?" The land meant everything to him. It had been in his family a long time. I always thought it would have been good for him to sell some of it because he had no income except the one hundred dollars per month that he received as a World War I pension. His offer put me in a state of shock.

Concerning the amount, he said, "How much do you want?" I really think he was prepared to give us whatever amount I requested, but I decided I would just step off farmer-style an amount which looked adequate for the building and parking space that we had anticipated needing for the future. We walked together and staked the corners of the plot that turned out to be about three and one-half acres with about 150 feet of road frontage. Later it was worked out with Mr. Green so that the church could own five and one-half acres. The church bought only two acres of that amount from him. Even when he sold two acres because he needed the money, he charged no interest and gave the church a clear title. The amount we staked off that day was valued at thirty-five thousand dollars by the banker when we applied for a loan to build the first permanent building.

Mr. Green's way of giving it to us was to put it in his will that we would receive ownership at his death. I knew that he did not intend to do anything with it in the meantime other than let us use it. In his mind, we could build on it regardless of whether we owned it or he owned it. That may sound strange to us now, but it was not strange to Mr. Green. His word was always his bond. I also knew that we could not do that as a church. I knew we must have ownership in order to build on the land and to use it for collateral in borrowing building money.

After hearing what I had to say about it, he decided he would go make a will, which he had not done up to that time, and also make the church a deed for the amount that we had stepped off. We had the land surveyed, and the deed was made within a few days. The land was actually deeded to the Congress Heights Baptist Church but became ours upon the organization of our church into a "duly organized Baptist church."

As far as we were concerned, that was the last big hurdle

to our continuing progress in the development of the church. Mr. Green's was the only land that had not already been subdivided for house lots in that area where the cost of land was rising every day. The gift of the land was a miracle.

Mr. Green was an unusual man. He had little formal education but always seemed to know what was happening around him and what he wanted from life. He never pressed for conversation but liked to talk when he could find a willing listener. He could be characterized as a gentle man because he rarely showed anger or even raised his voice unless upset by what he thought was unfair play in a televised wrestling match, which he loved to watch.

He talked slowly and laughed quickly. His family was his sister-in-law and, I believe, only one niece, one nephew, one great-niece, and three great-nephews. He apparently felt closest to his nephew, to whom he willed most, if not all, of his remaining land. He appeared to be easy to push around, but that just was not the case. He had character of steel, sensitivity, and compassion that made him appear to be a pushover. Anytime he heard of someone's misfortune, his eyes would cloud up with tears and he would be unable to speak. He lived all his life in the Fort Foote area. That was his only world with the exception of his experiences in France with the U.S. Cavalry in World War I. I never heard him called anything other than Uncle Jay or Mr. Green. This was more from respect than because of his age.

Giving the church thirty-five thousand dollars worth of land was as much in keeping with his philosophy of life as anything could possibly be. That was the reason he could do it so matter-of-factly in casual conversation as he had done that day in front of the feed building. I heard a seminary professor say once, "If searching for the greatest Christian who ever lived, it might be found in the elderly lady who walks down her farm house lane to get her mail known only by her family and a few close friends." I always felt Mr. Green was that kind of person. How appropriate that when the educational wing of the present Fort Foote church was built, it was named the Jay Green Educational Building. While the permanent building was under construction, he said, "Every day, to look from my kitchen window and see the construction of the new church is all that I could ever want out of life."

With a clear title deed to our land, we were now ready to talk rather than just think about a new building. However, the first thing we did was to remove the abandoned chicken house that was on our new property. Mr. Green had three rather large chicken houses, and none had been in use since his retirement. All provided the same pungent odor on a rainy day when the wind was blowing, but the one on our new property was the strongest. We tore it down. I do not recall all who helped at this job, but there were plenty of volunteers.

By now the congregation was averaging about 125 each Sunday, but we had little money. The operational expenses, including my salary and house rent, took up all that regular offerings. In keeping with our basic philosophy of a church, from the very beginning we gave 10 percent of our income to outside causes. This left little for a building fund.

From The Sunday School Board of the Southern Baptist Convention, we acquired architectural plans for the right kind of building in our situation. After thorough study by Sunday School Board architects, plans were given to us for a three-stage building program. It was practical to first build a chapel, then educational space, and then the permanent sanctuary. As practical as that plan was, it just wasn't possible for us to implement it. We had to have a first building that would allow us to grow. Naturally, we did want the most we could get with the amount of money we could obtain. In spite of the fact that we had used a fruit stand and a feed building for a worship place, because they were the best we could do at the time, we had always wanted something better.

We began to think of people we knew who were skilled in the building trades. We knew Wayne Sisson who had laid block for the little building we had provided Mr. Green in exchange for the feed building. We knew a plumber who would give us good work at a price as low as anyone and a home building contractor who lived near the church. The contractor said that he would be interested in looking at our plans, and the bricklayer and the plumber said they would be interested in subcontracting.

We proceeded to have plans drawn up for a building that would seat 325 for worship, with unfinished educational space that could accommodate nearly as many if every space were used, such as the pastor's study, the choir room, the vestibule, the sanctuary, and the unfinished basement. Now, this situation seemed totally inadequate and even unsatisfactory. But it seemed like a cathedral compared to our previous facilities.

These plans were drawn and submitted to three different contractors for closed bids. The bids ranged from forty thousand to sixty-five thousand dollars and the lowest was from Bill Rowe, the home contractor in the community, as we expected it would be. He had never built a building as large as our proposed building or one that cost that much. He had given us a "shoestring" bid, planning to use the subcontractors that we had contacted and as much free labor as we could provide. We knew this and our members did help as much as they could, but Bill, though he never complained, made very little profit from building our church.

We had plans and a builder but still no money. Forty thousand dollars seems like a rather small amount for a congregation of 125 to raise, but all the money they could give was needed for the operation and work of the church. Some

of our members had very little money to give for any purpose.

We did have two important factors in our favor for borrowing money. One was the ownership of thirty-five thousand dollars worth of land for collateral and the other was
the backing of the Congress Heights Baptist Church. They
could give no money or assume any part of our loan because
they were heavily in debt with their own building program;
but I am sure that their promise of support, if needed, had
some effect on the banker's willingness to lend us money.

Before trying the bank, we thought of all the sources that
might be available to us. One was Congress Heights Baptist
Church, another was the D.C. Baptist Convention, and still
another was the Church Loans Department of the Home
Mission Board of the Southern Baptist Convention. The
Congress Heights Church was ruled out immediately. We
next contacted the D.C. Baptist Convention.

From the beginning, we had been encouraged by the
leaders of the D.C. Baptist Convention but had not been
given any tangible support. The reason was that there were
several places in the Washington area based on population
that were considered more needy for a church, and certainly many situations appeared to be more likely to succeed
than ours did. I recall that we were about the twentieth on
the list for financial support, so our pitch to the convention
was that we were ready to build and the others were not at
that time. Of course, the convention was right in its priority
listing based on all the statistics and circumstances that must
determine sensibly and reasonably its priority listing. The
result was that we did not get any money for our proposed
building.

We next turned to the Home Mission Board's Church
Loan Department. We prepared detailed statistics, a back-
ground of our church, and complete plans for our building.
The response was that we were placed one hundred twen-

tieth on their priority list for financial help for almost the same reasons the D.C. convention had given. They, too, were right, and we still had no money for our proposed building.

We were sure that we could get some money from the bank but probably not nearly enough, yet there was nothing left to do but try. At the meeting of our church called for the purpose of discussing borrowing from the bank, one member came up with a suggestion. The suggestion was that any member who owned a home or property would assume responsibility for a specific amount of any loan the bank would give us by mortgaging their own property. This offer which covered approximately twenty thousand dollars of the loan was put in writing and included in the package that I was to present to the banker.

I had never gone before a banker to borrow money for anything other than a car, so I really didn't know what was needed in the package or even what approach to take. The bank that we went to for the loan was the one where Sara Redman worked as a teller. This was incidental to our going there but, as it turned out, was very significant.

I stated my purpose to the receptionist and asked to see the president of the bank. I was introduced to John Harris. In addition to being the president of the bank, he was a member and treasurer of a new Baptist church in Upper Marlboro in the greater Washington area where he lived. That made him sympathetic to our cause, though maybe more dubious to our situation because the approach of his group to building was very different from ours.

With some skepticism, he heard my story, looked at our plans, and asked about the cost of construction. I showed him all the bids, hoping to impress him with the fact that the building we were getting was really worth considerably more than the lowest bid of forty thousand dollars. He never commented but only asked how much of the forty thousand we wanted to borrow. I said, "Forty thousand" with as much assurance in my voice as I could manage. He said, "But you don't understand. Banks never lend more than two-thirds of the total cost of the building. Don't you have any money?"

We did have between four and five thousand dollars but would need that and more for furnishings and equipment not included in the construction cost. He already knew that our sponsoring church was in no financial situation to help us. We then discussed the value of our land and established it at thirty-five thousand dollars with full knowledge that it could only increase. I then injected the interest and sincerity of our members as manifested by their willingness to assume responsibility for specific amounts of the loan by mortgaging their homes. He did appear to be impressed by that.

He became very thoughtful. After considering every aspect of the proposal, he made a very surprising statement. "I am going to approve the loan. The determining factor, however, is the change in Sara Redman's life since she became a member of your church. That makes me believe in your ability to succeed more than your collateral."

I was very happy to get the promise of the forty thousand dollars, but even happier to hear him make that statement. The building money was not really as important as the witness of Sara's life.

8

A New Building on Our Own Land

Just a few days after the bank granted us the loan, the note was signed and preparations to build began. We had a ground-breaking ceremony with the pastor of Congress Heights Baptist Church, a D.C. convention representative, and all of our members who wanted to participate.

Because our church seemed to get more done from a strong group spirit, it seemed appropriate for each member to turn a shovel of dirt. The youngest children were included. Interest in the construction of the new building was as high among the young people of the church as it was among the adults. I think participating in the ground-breaking ceremony made them continue to feel a part of what was happening.

When the bulldozer arrived to begin leveling the site and digging the basement, people were there to watch. Observing the construction was as moving as raising a flag. We grew personally with every phase of the construction. As we observed the work, we seemed to be inspired to do something with our lot in life. We had all dreamed about a new building someday, but it hardly seemed possible in less than three years from the time we first met in the fruit stand. Nearly every day someone would stop by to see how it was going. It took very little promotional talk to get our people involved in the life of the church. Construction of the building created more excitement than words ever could.

Mr. Green was now fully retired and spent most of his day

around the church. When he was not on the site, he was sitting by his kitchen window or leaning on a fence post. A sparkle in his eyes showed he was thinking what God, through the church, had done for him during the past two years. He felt fulfilled as a person and as a Christian. His spirit was contagious.

Seeing a permanent structure go up had an effect on the community. We had gained considerable respect and influence, but some were still skeptical about the feed building not being "churchy" enough for worship. Now, the church was really becoming permanent in the mind of the community. I soon began to be asked to participate as a minster in civic programs. This was another step in community relations that resulted from having a new building on our own land.

With this giant step forward, there came many growing pains. Attendance was increasing, enthusiasm was running high, and new people were coming in at a little faster rate than before. We had always had a quality worship service, but our educational program was not on the same level. We had some very well-qualified and excellent teachers and leaders, but others were not so qualified. We did not provide training for any of the teachers and leaders of our Sunday School. The qualified did well, but some accomplished little and did not have the respect of their classes.

In the beginning, most of our members had little church background and even less knowledge of the Bible. They willingly did their best, but their limitations were beginning to have a direct effect on the educational program of the church. The answer was to have someone qualified give the training we needed. There was no one in our church who had the qualifications and experience that we needed to do this for us, so we began to look elsewhere. On previous occasions when such a need arose in our music program, we were able to get help in Bill Richards from our sponsoring church. We again turned to them.

I have stated earlier that their pastor was more enthusiastic about starting new churches than anyone I have ever known. Anytime he heard of anyone interested in starting churches, he would contact them whether he really had anything for them to do or not. The pastor suggested we consider Spurgeon Dewitt Swinney, Jr., who from this point will be called "Spud."

Spud was about thirty years old, unmarried, from Oklahoma, a recent graduate of Southwestern Baptist Theological Seminary in Texas, and a member of the Tentmakers organization. The Tentmakers was an organization sponsored by the Home Mission Board of the Southern Baptist Convention for people who wanted to do mission work and were willing to earn their own living through secular work.

Al Smith, the Congress Heights pastor, had given his name as a contact person to the Home Mission Board for Tentmakers who wanted to work in the Washington area. When Spud contacted him, Al said to come, "Because we need you in this area." Spud came with the understanding that, when he arrived, a secular job would be waiting for him and some mission work would soon get under way. He arrived in Washington in an old Buick that barely made it. He had little money and no job. He was a person of sterling character, a strong commitment to his calling as a minister, a well-trained and capable leader.

There was always much going on at Congress Heights Baptist Church which took the time of the leaders. This particular time was no exception. Spud couldn't get the help he needed to find secular work. The pastor told me about his plight. We felt he was just the person we needed to help with our educational program. Spud was qualified and well trained but his main interests were in preaching and singing. He did both exceptionally well but was willing to do what the situation demanded. When I approached him with our need, he agreed.

A couple in our church worked for the Post Office Department and helped Spud get a job sorting mail. He accepted the office of Sunday School superintendent where he could lead and train as needed. Spud's coming to help us marked a major turning point and advancement in our educational program and the overall work of the church.

He was overqualified for the work he was doing but did it without complaint and with genuine enthusiasm. He became a vital church member and a close family friend. Being a bachelor, he was a good cook and often offered to help prepare the food when he was having a meal with us. He stayed with us until after our organizational service the following year when he accepted the pastorate of a church in Port Deposit, Maryland.

As our building came closer to completion, we tried to be patient. I doubt that Bill Rowe, the contractor, thought we were trying very hard. We wanted to have our first service on Easter Sunday. As is always the case, there were holdups in the building process that only the builder can understand. When progress was slowed, we offered to help because we just had to have the building ready for worship by Easter.

As that time approached, it was evident that the main structure of the building could be completed, but the interior would not be painted, and there would be no pews or heat. None of this made a difference to us because we could just transfer our folding chairs, and it looked better without paint than what we had and, hopefully, the weather would be such that we would not need heat. However, just in case it was a cold day, we would temporarilty install our old space heater. With much encouragement, some prodding, and a little help for the builder, the building was sufficiently completed for us to meet on Easter 1958. We had done a lot of promoting and inviting and had our largest attendance up to that time.

The attendance was large, but the conditions were miserable. All the warmth of spirit and enthusiasm that we could muster just could not raise the low temperature of the building. Heat from our transferred space heater was negligible in this larger space. Not only was the space heater ineffective but also the temporary arrangement caused the heater to expel more oil fumes than ever before. We had been over anxious and were paying for it on Easter morning. In spite of the miserable conditions, we felt good about being there, and the visitors seemed to understand and shared our feeling of gratitude.

In talking with the banker, I had indicated that we had between four and five thousand dollars we hoped to save to buy furnishings and equipment for our new building. The reason I could not be specific was that about twelve hundred dollars of it was pledge money. Our faith in those who pledged was such that a committee had gone to a church furniture company in North Carolina to select and place our order.

When we first began planning, we knew that we would need every penny we could get just for the building. Any money for furnishings was going to be difficult to obtain. During this period, a lot of new housing developments were going up in southeast Washington. Old buildings, including church buildings, were being torn down and new buildings constructed. Some churches were selling their buildings and furnishings and relocating in different areas. We decided that we might be able to obtain some pews from some of them. We preferred new furniture but might have to be satisfied with used. We investigated the possibility of used pews and pulpit furniture. We found some we could live with and placed a sealed bid, as required, but did not get the pews. We tried this with another church but failed again.

We gave up on that plan and began to think in terms of raising more money so we could buy all new furnishings. We had learned that each pew was going to cost ninety-five dollars. We would need at least twenty to begin with and ten more later to fill the sanctuary.

We had always followed the practice that every member should feel a responsibility to the church, and that included the young people. By this time we had several teenagers, most of whom were still in school. Some had graduated and were working. Many of them were active in church, even though their parents didn't come. One day a teenager was telling me how proud and grateful he was for the church. It occurred to me that the young people would be a good source for the pew money. I decided I would ask each one of them to buy one pew. They would not have to give all the money at once but could pledge and give an amount each week that would total the ninety-five dollars by the time it was needed. I was hesitant to do this because I did not want to hurt anyone's relationship with the church if he did not have the money or did not want to contribute.

I contacted Walter Calhoun first. He was one of the working teenagers who had recently joined the church through baptism. His brother attended church, but his parents did not. I explained the plan to him and asked if he would like to participate. Much to my surprise, he reached in his pocket, pulled out a roll of money, and handed me the ninety-five dollars for a pew. Before two weeks had passed we had either cash or pledges for twelve of the twenty pews, all from teenage young people.

When the youth of the church were offered a responsible role, they responded accordingly. To me, this was evidence that real participation does far more to maintain their interest than anything that the church might do for them. They have more to offer, even in financial ways, than adults often suspect.

When the new pews were installed, we installed an attractive desk for the pastor's study and a quality organ for the sanctuary. The desk was of heavy oak that Al and Libby Mers bought somewhere, refinished, and gave to the church. After twenty-five years, it is still being used and is nicer looking than many desks one might see in a pastor's study.

The organ was bought for the church by Mary and Monty Montgomery. They gave the down payment and made the monthly payments until the church was financially able to make them, which was about one year after purchase, as I recall.

The Mers family had started attending our church just about the time we began meeting in the feed building. Their close friends, the Montgomerys, were quality Christians with good judgment and ability. Monty was the treasurer and a good, steady influence in the church. Mary was an excellent organist and served in that capacity during the entire time they were with us. Al and Libby Mers could do most anything that needed to be done. They were two of our most valuable families during the time they were with us.

Soon we were ready for the building dedication. The building was symbolic of God's blessings. It represented many miracles and much human achievement. The dedication of it was very important to all of us.

Al Smith was there to represent the Congress Heights Baptist Church. Bill Crowder, director of missions and evangelism for the D.C. convention, and Bill Rowe, the general contractor, participated in the program. M. Ray McKay, my professor of preaching from Southeastern Seminary, preached the dedication sermon. Friends and family gathered for a very special and meaningful service and a very happy day for the Fort Foote Baptist Church. I presided, but tears and the fear of losing control made speaking difficult. Somehow they seemed appropriate to express the gratitude

I felt. Much was said about who was involved and how much had happened to make possible this building in a little less than three years. My mind kept going back to twelve members in need of God's help and the first meeting in a fruit stand.

Upon completion of the building, we set our minds to beautifying the grounds. The area around the church had been cleared and graded, but there was no grass or shrubbery. The feed building still stood very nearly in front of the new building. There was some nostalgia involved, but we decided to take it down. The yard was sodded and shrubs planted. A parking area was provided at one side and in back of the church. A driveway entrance at one corner of the property extended to the parking area and exited at the opposite corner.

Building and grounds finally were in good shape. Now all we needed was a nice sign out front. With finances depleted and all income spoken for by building payments and operational expenses, someone suggested an inexpensive way to get the sign. A member working on a construction job in the city had an idea. We obtained a concrete slab for the footing, got Wayne Sisson to do the brick work, another member did the glass work, and the sign that is still out front today was completed at low cost.

The only difficult part was transporting the concrete slab from downtown Washington to the church. We borrowed a member's pickup truck and went to get it. It must have weighed well over a ton. This was much more than the truck was made to carry. We loaded it with a crane at the site, but we had no crane at the church. We somehow managed to get the truck out from under it and let it drop into the hole that had been prepared for it. The slab was so heavy that the front wheels of the truck touched the ground only for about half of the two hours it took to get to the church. The young truck driver was another in a long series of people who was willing to try something he had never done before. Fortunately, the truck was not damaged and no accident occurred during the trip.

The Thomas Addison Elementary School was located just a short distance from Indian Head Highway, close to the District of Columbia boundary. It had been there for a few years. Children from most of the Fort Foote area attended the school even though it was not really in the Fort Foote community. The first school that was built in the immediate community was the Fort Foote Elementary School. It was located across the road from the corner grocery and garage. The building of this school showed how the population of the community was growing and what was anticipated in the future. Within what I have described as the geographic boundary of the community was now a garage, a grocery, a church, and a school, giving it a legitimate community status that it had not had before. The community seemed to be following the same pattern of development as the church.

In planning the new building, we had first included all that a church building with a seating capacity of three hundred and twenty-five should have. This would include a baptistry and a kitchen because Baptists always baptize their converts, and many like to eat as often as they can at the church. Due to lack of money, however, we first had to eliminate the kitchen and then the baptistry. We had always gone to the sponsoring church and baptized at an evening service, so we felt we could continue to do that until some plan could be found to build our own baptistry. As long as I was there, plans for our own baptistry were often suggested, but none ever materialized.

We had plenty of parking space and the graded driveway but had not been able to afford having it paved or even graveled. The driveway was packed very hard and was usable but very slippery on rainy days. This was just one other important project that had to wait.

9
The Church Grows

Barbara Prinkey had tried very hard to get her parents to come with her to church. Her mother would come occasionally, but her father never did. I had visited him more than once to invite and encourage him to come. None of our efforts had been successful. One morning after the service had started, Mr. Prinkey walked into the church. I knew this had to be a very satisfying moment for Barbara. I suppose I was almost as pleased as she was happy. She was happy to see her father in church; I was pleased to see my friend.

The only problem I had with his being there for the first time was that I was planning to preach on stewardship. I just knew a money sermon was not a proper one for a man like Mr. Prinkey. Barbara had worked so hard to get him to church, and now I was about to ruin it. I had not heard him say so, but many outside the church often say "money is the only reason they want me to come anyway." I panicked. But I had no other sermon. So I went ahead with the one I had prepared, regardless of how much I wanted to change it.

I dreaded to greet him at the door after the service was over. But there was no choice. When he came by me, I gave a usual greeting and expressed appreciation for his coming. He responded with a real shocker. He said, "I notice your driveway has not been surfaced, and I would like to do that for you. I cannot afford to blacktop it, but I will provide the gravel for it and have a truck deliver it next week if you want me to." The total cost was probably about one hundred dollars. Never again have I been reluctant to discuss money from the pulpit, though I must admit I have never since gotten that kind of instant results.

With Sara Redman, Bill Richards, Dolly Sherman, Spud Swinney, and Mary Montgomery, we had always had quality music for our services. Dolly was still with us to sing in the choir and to sing solos. The choir had been started the first Sunday in the new building. Mary consistently provided good organ music. The others had gone, and we now had no choir director. When Bill was our music director, we had given him a token amount of money which probably covered little more than travel expense from his home to the church three times a week. We still could not afford more and a volunteer would have to be found. There was none avilable from our own congregation, so again we turned to our sponsoring church.

Roger Dodson was one of their faithful choir members. Their director had told me that Roger might be interested in coming to serve with us. He had not directed a choir before but was certainly the kind of person who would do his best if he accepted the responsibility. I approached Roger about our need. After some deliberation, he decided to come. Under Roger's leadership, the choir developed into as fine a church choir as I have ever seen for a church that size. Roger selected good music, and the choir always presented it well.

One morning after they had sung routinely, I noticed a man, who was a rather hardened individual, wiping tears from his eyes. Not knowing that I had observed him that day, he later told me, "The presentation by the choir this morning was one of the most moving experiences of my life." After we left the church and were living in Japan, recordings of the choir were sent to us. Hearing the choir again brought tears to our eyes much as it had done to the hardened man in the congregation that morning.

The choir during Roger's time as music director was certainly a very positive factor in the development of the Fort Foote Baptist Church. Somehow those with little experience who came to serve in leadership roles seemed to develop right along with the church. This was true with Roger Dodson. I attribute that to the fact that such people had sound character along with a strong commitment to God and to their church responsibilities.

We had always known that some day we would actually have to have a special organizational service for the purpose of becoming an "organized Baptist church" but talked little about it. We told ourselves and all who would listen that we were as much a church from the first day that we met in a little prayer and Bible study group as we would ever be. We really believed the church to be an organism and not an organization. Regardless of how small the organism, it was still the church. Having a service for the purpose of organizing in order to become a church seemed contradictory. It was true that we were listed by the Congress Heights Baptist Church and the D.C. convention as a mission. We had always cooperated and allowed ourselves to be thought of by the mother church and the convention as a mission. We appreciated very much the help they provided in our development.

The relationship was not always positive, however. At their request, we had always reported our Sunday School attendance and offering to be included in their bulletin. One Sunday, during the period of time that they were giving me twenty-five dollars per month, there was a typographical error that reflected our offering to be a hundred dollars less than it actually was. I never did like to give the report because I did not like to be considered a mission, but I went along with the idea. When this error occurred, however, it just gave me the opportunity to do what I had always wanted to do, which was to stop giving the report.

So I called the pastor and said, "We are not going to be giving the report any more. It reflects badly on us even when it is right and to make such an error as has been made is something that we will not tolerate." He replied over the phone, "Well, in that case you won't get the twenty-five dollars anymore." I said, in a very angry tone, "That's fine with me. Just consider the relationship between your church and our mission severed," and hung up.

Though I was wrong, at the time I meant exactly what I had said. We would never accept help from anyone if it meant compromising in any way our philosophy or our independence as a church. In less than one hour, the pastor was at my door and convinced me that typographical errors should never be a reason to sever a relationship between two churches. It would be good for both of us to continue the report and the receiving of money.

By the summer of 1959, along with the Congress Heights Baptist Church and the D.C. convention, we felt it was time to have the organizational service. In spite of our lack of enthusiasm for the need of it, it was a very meaningful service. Somehow, in that service, it got through to me that there is something very good and very Christian about cooperating with others. I believe that it might have been the beginning of a spirit that I hope has characterized my ministry since that time.

Our next step was to apply for admission to the District of Columbia Baptist Convention. This involved representatives of our church going before a convention committee to answer questions and present our story. Then, at the annual meeting in November, the convention would vote on the recommendation of the committee.

Russell Lefebre was chosen to go with me to appear before the convention committee. Russell had been a member since the early days in the feed house, was teacher of our men's Sunday School class, one of our most articulate and respected members, and obviously a good choice to represent the congregation. We were asked to give the usual statistics of membership and offerings, financial situation, prospects for the future, and reasons why our church wanted to become a member of the convention.

At first, there was stony silence like going before the bank to get a building loan. But gradually, they began to see how our church had developed through unusual circumstances and against heavy odds. Interest grew. Reverend Archibald, pastor of the Chevy Chase Baptist Church, finally exclaimed, "This is like a chapter out of the Book of Acts!" The committee was amazed to hear that a man like Mr. Green would give such high-priced land and feel good about it. Reverend Archibald asked if he might use in a sermon Mr. Green's statement, "This is all I want out of life."

At the annual meeting, the church was accepted as a member of the District of Columbia Baptist Convention and has been a cooperating and participating member since that time.

In the summer of 1959, the church decided to buy a parsonage. We had been living in a house rented from one of the members for almost three years. The monthly payment was little more than we were paying for rent and only a $2,500 down payment was required. The church decided that would be a good investment. After a special business meeting, upon recommendation from the trustees, the church voted to purchase the three-bedroom house that is still used for the parsonage. The only real problem in the decision was that we did not have the down payment and could not afford to obligate ourselves further with payments on a second mortgage.

Mr. Roberts did not attend church very often, but we had become good friends through my visits in their home with Mrs. Roberts, one of the first twelve members. One day we were discussing this parsonage opportunity and the problem of the down payment and he said, "I have some money that I would be glad to lend you." I told him the church just could not afford more monthly payments at this time. He said, "I did not mean that I would lend it to the church. I meant that I would lend it to you, as my friend." I couldn't make the payment then and, besides, I had no collateral. He said, "I know that. But this is my offer. I will lend you the twenty-five hundred dollars with no interest if you will not reveal to anyone except Frances the source of it. You and Frances can sign a statement that you will pay me back whenever you can. You will be solely responsible for deciding when that will be."

This was an unexpected, unbelievable offer that was almost too good to be true. Mr. Roberts was not a professing Christian at that time, and I was not sure it was good judgment to accept the offer from him. I wondered, too, how I could handle the secrecy with the church. The church knew that Frances and I had no money and would almost assuredly wonder how we had gotten it. I did know Mr. Roberts well, and I knew him to be a very private person whose word was literally his bond. He may have had many faults but dishonesty in any form was not one of them. I decided to accept his offer and asked the church to go ahead and consider the trustees' recommendation with the understanding that the down payment would come from an anonymous source and that I would be responsible for it until such time that the church decided it could afford to include it along with their building loan responsibility.

At Mr Robert's funeral service just two years ago, which I conducted, Mrs. Roberts gave me permission to reveal that Mr. Roberts was the source of that parsonage down payment. He made a public profession of faith shortly after I left and became a member of the church. But as far as I know, Frances, Mrs. Roberts, and I are the only ones who knew about the loan until the day of the funeral.

It seemed that there was always some generous person around to meet whatever basic need related to the development of the church. The land, the building, some furnishings, the organ, the parsonage—all had been purchased with generosity from unexpected people and unsolicited.

Now it was Mr. Green's turn again. During another casual conversation, he said he would like to make sure through a will that the church would never have any land problem. So he changed his will to provide up to a total of five and one-half acres for the church.

Mr. Green's monthly income was still only the pension he was receiving for World War I service. The church decided to give him one hundred dollars per month as an additional source of income, which he needed badly but would never have requested. A gift from him was always a "love gift." There was never an obligation from the receiver. With this additional land, the church had acquired in less than five years all the basic property needed for present and future development.

The physical part of the church development was essential, but the people development part was even more important. This was demonstrated through Mrs. Snead and her Sunday School class. She and her class members called it the "Old Ladies Class." Mrs. Snead was the oldest member of this class. As a teacher, she was their leader and inspiration.

I believe she had heard about the meetings through the Redmans who were Herman's friends. The church was then meeting in the fruit stand. Most of the time before Herman and Mabel started attending regularly, Mrs. Snead would get a ride from a friend. Sometimes she would ride the city bus about one hour to the District boundary where someone from our church picked her up and brought her the rest of the way to church. By some means, she would always be present at the main church meetings. The fact that she lived on Rhode Island Avenue, Northwest, and the church was located in Maryland beyond the southeast corner of the District was never a problem to her.

Mrs. Snead's husband died during the depression years of the thirties, leaving her with five small children. She had no earning skills. Soon after her husband's death, she managed to earn a degree in practical nursing.

She always saw the bright side of everything. With her, dullness in any form was almost detestable. She dressed in bright colors and could make any situation lively if by nothing more than her presence. She would have nothing to do with alcoholic beverages, so I was surprised when she invited us to her apartment for Christmas dinner to find her beautifully prepared table with a glass of what I thought was red wine at each plate. Soon I learned the glasses were filled with red Kool-Aid for the purpose of providing some color for the table.

Her optimism was demonstrated once when she invited us to go home with her after church for dinner. She assured us that she had plenty of food to include our family in the Sunday meal. Later she revealed that she actually had made no preparation. In fact, she had no food in the house for a dinner for guests and no money to buy any. By chance, Herman and Mabel accepted an invitation to join us and offered to bring with them some food that they had already prepared. Mrs. Snead accepted, and there was sufficient food for all of us.

The most significant part of that story is not that Mrs. Snead had no food and no money, but the reason she had no money. She was working as a practical nurse and earning an average income by nursing elderly people in their homes. On the day she invited us for Sunday dinner, she had signed her salary check and given it to the church. I do not know how often she did this, but I do know that the offerings from her Sunday School class were often higher than any other class. Anytime extra money was needed, she would suggest that we not worry about it because it would most likely be available from some source. That source was more often than not herself. Others never knew of her generosity to the church. Her enthusiasm was contagious. In her own way, though she held no office other than Sunday School teacher, she was one of the most effective leaders.

One thing Mrs. Snead did that was noticeable was to get members of her family to start attending the church. As a result of her influence, I baptized eight members of her family. These included two sons, a daughter, a son-in-law and daughter, a granddaughter and her fiance. She never used pressure tactics but would do considerable maneuvering. Often she contacted me in order to get others interested in the church. Through Mrs. Snead, the church was very helpful to members of her family and to many of their friends. The church was her life. Through the church, she saw her prayers answered and experienced great fulfillment as she served God. She is still a member and, though in her late eighties, is able to attend on a fairly regular basis.

When I applied for entrance in the seminary, I was accepted on the condition that before time for graduation, I would obtain twelve more liberal arts college hours. This was required because all my previous academic training had been in the physical sciences and did not give me the number of liberal arts hours required for admission to the seminary. I was busy enough my first two free summers being a full-time pastor that I had neglected to get these needed hours. I had to do that before I could begin my third year of seminary studies. I enrolled in the University of Maryland and got the hours required in one semester. Due to a problem in scheduling, I had to wait until the following year to complete my degree from the seminary. That year of waiting was the only complete year out of the six that I was actually a full-time pastor. All the other years I was either in the Air Force or the seminary.

Graduating from seminary was the highlight of my academic career, which included a total of nine years after high school. When I walked before the president to receive the degree, it was a very emotional moment. The theological education and total seminary experience were life-changing for me, but that was one of the smaller reason for the feeling. This seemed more like a church and family achievement than my own. The church had provided the necessary financial support and encouragement. They had also been patient with my maturing process as a preacher and pastor.

The emotional part of the experience of walking before the president for the degree also related to Frances and our two children. When I graduated, Anna was six and Robert was four. I had taken them some small gift each Friday when I returned home, but that was only token and no substitute for their having no father at home with them five days of each week for three years. Their sacrifice was much more than mine.

Of course, the real burden of my seminary training was on Frances. Being mother and father for two small children and pastor of a church like ours during that time was considerably more than what she had anticipated when she married chemist Carrol Bruce nine years before. I often wonder, *How did she do it?* After the graduation ceremony, Frances took a picture of Robert wearing my graduation cap. To this day, it is one of my most cherished photographs. My graduation was truly a family achievement.

By April 1961, Fort Foote Baptist Church had grown to two hundred sixty-five, with an active congregation of at least three hundred. They were all present for the Easter service. At the normal morning worship services, the church appeared full—meaning probably about 250. On that day, the pews were packed and extra folding chairs were placed in the aisle.

The church was a large part of our life, but Frances and

I had always said that we would remain open to any work
that we felt right for us. We never liked to feel that God only
spoke once even as it related to a life's work. We never
discussed anything in particular but always wanted to be
open to any new calling.

In keeping with what we interpreted as being integral in
the purpose of the church, foreign missions was very important. We had regular foreign missions emphases by having
missionary speakers and making financial contributions. A
mission spirit had prompted the beginning of the Fort Foote
Baptist Church. It was just natural for me to hear with open-
ness missionary speakers who came from time to time to the
seminary.

During my first year at seminary, a personnel secretary
for the Southern Baptist Foreign Mission Board spoke and
interviewed individuals interested in foreign missions. With
probably more than the usual pastor's interest in missions,
I made an appointment to talk with him. At that meeting,
I related my interest and told him that I did feel some sense
of leadership in the direction of foreign mission service. He
and I discussed how to interpret a call and left it at that, with
a promise from him that he would not discuss our meeting
with anyone else. I did not want to influence Frances who
would have to feel the same call as I did. She was capable
of deciding for herself how her life was to be used, but it is
natural for a husband or wife to be influenced by the other's
feeling.

I had no further meetings with a Foreign Mission Board
representative, and I never told Frances or anyone else
about the 1957 meeting. For the next three years, however,
I did experience a growing concern and interest in foreign
missions and felt very willing to be a missionary. Any decision for us to become foreign missionaries would have to be
instigated by Frances. I did not really feel this was a possibil-

ity because we had never discussed becoming foreign missionaries.

The possibility of our becoming missionaries became more likely in December 1960. We were having the annual foreign missions emphasis with a missionary speaker. On our way home from church, Frances said she thought we should consider missionary service. I was surprised and delighted. From that time, we both seemed to become more and more positive that we should apply to the Foreign Mission Board for appointment as foreign missionaries. We did. Within four months, we were given indefinite appointments to serve in Japan. It was rather fast, but we had met all the requirements, including pastoral experience. We were actually appointed three weeks before I graduated from the seminary.

Immediately after we applied and were given serious consideration by the board, we told the church that we would be leaving, if appointed. The church seemed shocked at the news but appreciated the opportunity to share with us the process of appointment that sometimes could be rather lengthy. We were appointed in a ceremony in Richmond, Virginia, with a large part of our congregation in attendance. Again, we felt this was something that our church was as much involved in as we were. They had been very much a part of the growth that had brought us to make the decision.

The church was very kind through many expressions of love presented to us at a farewell dinner given in our honor prior to our last Sunday with them. The dinner was held in the fellowship hall of the Congress Heights Baptist Church in order to accommodate all our members. I believe they were just about all there. It was a very wonderful occasion but very sad from the standpoint of our leaving. We had been the only pastor's family that a large number of them had ever known. More importantly, we had struggled together, tried the impossible together, and enjoyed unexpected victories together. We were a part of each other. I do not remember the food that was served, but I do remember the program. It was well planned to include humor and substance, but it could only be described as empty. We all went through the motions of eating and doing our part on the program, but our minds were already on parting.

Our last Sunday with the church was different. I did not attempt to preach but spoke only briefly to express gratitude for the love they had shown us. I think our real feeling in leaving was that we were leaving friends rather than just church members. Not much was said, but a lot was felt.

In our leaving, a nearly six-year era in the life of the church passed. In the next few years, the church was to continue with even more rapid growth. The Jay Green Educational Building was built.

We arrived in Japan in August of that year to begin our new work and a new life. I must point out that as involved as we were, Frances says it took at least three years for me to get the Fort Foote people out of my regular thoughts. They had become truly a part of our lives. "Seek ye first the kingdom of God, and his righteousness; and all these things shall be added unto you" (Matt. 6:33), no doubt was written for individuals but was never fulfilled more completely than through the Fort Foote Baptist Church.

As much as I tried to stay out of the Air Force and as much as I tried to get out after I was in it, the Air Force played a very large role in the development of the church. Because of my Air Force salary, we were able to work with the church for two years without any financial support from the church. I might add that my salary was higher than other officers of equal rank because I had been commissioned longer. This was very adequate for comfortable living and considerably more than most beginning preachers would have thought of receiving as salary. This meant we did not have to seek money first from the church in order to live so that we could do the work. We could always be low key about it because the Air Force was providing. This had nothing to do with our dedication or commitment, but it did prevent the usual skeptics from saying that the main purpose of the preacher is to get money. It was a strong factor in getting the church started. In this case, what I thought was our greatest hindrance to my calling was really our greatest help. Not the help I had planned, but the one God had in mind. At least, it was an example of his capacity to turn something believed to be bad into something unquestionably good.

No more need be said about the gift of the land making it possible for us to build the permanent building except that no other way seemed possible. It just had to be that God raised up a most unlikely man to do this for us. Unlikely, to me, because I have known so many wealthy land owners who would never even have thought of giving the land to a group like ours. This is so clear to me because the Mount Pisgah church where I grew up was about one and one-half miles from the closest hard-surfaced road. Long after the church needed a paved road and was able to provide it, the man who owned the farm that the road would have to go through would not consider even selling a right-of-way to the church, much less give it. It was not until after his death that the church, through his heirs, was able to have the right-of-way and build a road. Until that time, on rainy days we parked the cars on the main road and walked the remainder of the way. Yes, it was very unlikely to me that a man would give land for the building of a church.

The Air Force and Mr. Green were the big sources of needed money, but there were others as well. Some of the sources may not be acceptable to more pious Christians, but the money they provided did boost morale. For example, the extra offering that we received from crap game winnings of a visitor or the money given by unaffiliated church members and non-Christians not only boosted morale but also helped to pay bills at a time when it was needed.

The sponsoring church gave directly only twenty-five dollars per month for about two years, but their promise to stand behind our bank loan meant a lot of money to us because it suggested security to us as well as to the bank. The action of the bank itself in lending the total amount of the construction cost was not only unusual but also necessary, or we could not have built at the time we did. God's hand was evident in the president of the bank and in his statement relating to the changed life of Sara Redman.

The opportunity to assume a government loan on the parsonage was the means of getting a good house long before the church could have otherwise afforded it. That loan, which is very little now, is the only debt that the church has left. The reason is that the low interest rate made it wise to pay all other loans off first. Mr. Roberts, who provided the down payment money for the parsonage, made the purchase possible. Giving all by a committed member and the always sacrificial giving by so many who appeared to have so little just had to be sources that only God knew about and could provide as a way of adding to us what we needed when we needed it.

The Forte Foote Baptist Church was begun and developed the first six years of its history with little more than commitment of a few unlikely people. They were not theologians, but they came to know much about God.

The membership records now reflect 569 members. Since the beginning, as with most churches, there have been highs and lows in the various aspects of the church's growth and development, but this is the highest membership in its history.

I do not know when the church received the first black member. At present, the congregation is racially integrated to the extent that there are more black members than white.

70656

This racial change in the membership and leadership has corresponded to the racial change of the community. To my knowledge, there was never a serious problem related to this change. The church continues to be for the people of the community just as it was in its beginning. I feel that the Fort Foote Baptist Church, as established through the work of an unlikely twelve, has indeed been the work of God and will continue to be as long as its membership remains faithful to their commitment to be his people.

10
An Interpretation
Joel T. Land

There are many reasons the Fort Foote Baptist Church grew under the leadership of pastor Carrol Bruce. While his experience only happened once, many of these dynamics are at work in every new church. This final chapter is an attempt to define new work principles active in the Fort Foote experience.

The pastor himself is the most important human variable in every church start. Every successful new church start has a pastor or series of pastors who are certain of their calling and feel driven toward the pastoral ministry by God. The pastor must have a strong need to be a pastor. Only spiritual motivation from a source outside of himself is sufficient to keep him going through many difficult moments. His satisfaction from service becomes contagious.

Location is also an important element in a successful new church start. The area selected for the Fort Foote church was an undeveloped section at the metropolitan fringe of Washington, D.C. The vision and insight of the sponsoring church in locating a work in that area greatly contributed to its development as new people moved into the area. Developing metropolitan fringes and small towns have proved to be the most responsive locations for new churches.

Often the first core group of people in a new church will respond to a crisis ministry. They find help is available for their personal needs through the ministry of the pastor and people. Then they become Christians and finally Baptists.

Because of the chaotic lives of these crisis people, many do not initially feel at home in a regular church building. Temporary building facilities provide neutral ground on which they can come to church without being turned away by the holiness of its structure.

The pastor immediately found the most successful way to reach people is through ministry to friends and relatives of the core group. Word-of-mouth advertising was most effective in a small community. He discovered people networks and pursued them. Families brought their friends and relatives who needed help.

Pastors often get discouraged when the first people to respond to a new church seem to have little leadership potential. Most new Christians take time to get their lives together and do not immediately assume leadership roles. Twenty-five years later only one or two of the original twelve members are still active in the Fort Foote church. However, the church has grown to a membership of more than five hundred. One may conclude that the leadership potential of the beginning group is not as critical an issue as it is often thought.

In the Fort Foote church, leaders came after the church gained forty to fifty people. Mature Baptists moving into the area did not start joining the church until it had permanent facilities. One may conclude that a strong pastor can build a new church without strong local leaders in the beginning if he stays with the project five to six years. People develop leadership ability and mature church members join after the community becomes convinced the church has survived its beginning days.

But the new congregation must start with somebody. It may not matter who the somebodies are. Therefore, a pastor should minister more freely to whatever group is available if he knows stronger families will develop as the church grows.

Another critical element in church growth is a sense of movement and progress in the congregation. New people kept coming because miracles were taking place in the lives of the church members. These changes and conversions were shared with the congregation. Celebration of victories took place on a regular basis. Testimony time in a worship service and sharing of answered prayer tended to keep a high level of excitement in the congregation. This also kept the pastor encouraged and confident, as he offered Christ to people with radical hurts. When a pastor feels the church is being what it should be spiritually, he remains positive and vibrant in his own ministry. His positive attitude encourages other church members to share with their friends and relatives the excitement of what is happening.

The pastor was viewed as a well-rounded man. He was not afraid of manual labor. He enjoyed playing softball with the church members. At the same time, he had a strong interest in music. This meant that he knew good music and was able to find people in the congregation and in the mother church who could assist with worship. He discovered skills and interests in every person he met which could be offered as a gift to the church. There was not any skill or talent that could not in some way be used to benefit the work of Christ. The church members began to sense their own personal worth, as they were able to exercise their skills for a positive purpose.

This sense of well-being and fulfillment also contributed to the sense of movement and accomplishment in the church. People need to feel that their lives are going somewhere. This is usually accomplished by small successes, as well as a future orientation toward larger goals. The new church very much provided them a feeling of doing something important.

In addition to calling for personal gifts, the pastor did not hesitate to ask the people to give money. He knew the personal blessings of tithing and the spiritual dimensions of money management. Therefore, at critical times the people rose to meet financial needs. The church developed with very little outside financial support. The pastor and some of the members also had a business sense about handling finances so that they regularly got the most for their money. This created a sense of trust from the other members of the congregation. People will give if they feel their money is being used wisely for important needs.

Another strong reason that the church grew is that the pastor's wife had a ministry to certain groups in the church. In effect, they had two pastors. This was particularly true when he was out of town going to the seminary. They did not get in each other's way but complemented each other well. The people saw them functioning successfully as a family which provided a strong role model for the many chaotic marriages of the beginning group. A person does need to see a successful marriage taking place in order to know how one is done. Seeing a good family in action helped them to respect the opinions of the pastor when he did counseling or preached on family themes.

The childhood experiences of the pastor developed habits that were particularly valuable later in his life as a minister. For example, he learned to set goals each day which would move toward completing a project. He remembered plowing rows of corn and competing against his own best efforts. He had received approval from his family. After being successful in daily tasks, he also expected appreciation from the members of the church. Everyone needs approval. He found positive, constructive ways to secure approval of his work.

One of the most helpful lessons from his past was that he always seemed to have a *plan B*. If the first attempt at reaching a goal did not work, he always had a second or third way to go about accomplishing a critical task. Failure did not mean the end of a matter at all. It only meant it was time to try a new or alternative method.

The pastor himself feels that his strongest contribution was commitment. He originally called this book *A Commitment Happening* and sought to show how his own personal commitment and that of the original twelve members were the central reasons for its success. His personal honor kept him going against all odds. Once he had decided to be a pastor, his decision was severely tested, but there was never any question as to whether he would be a pastor. Once he had decided to start the new church, many obstacles had to be overcome. But in his mind there was never any question whether the church would succeed or not. He was able to communicate this confidence successfully to the new congegation.

Slowly, but certainly, the church became the life of its members. They lived in order to go to church. The church fulfilled their social needs, their need to be involved with other people, and their need to express themselves in a positive manner. The church proclaimed the forgiveness of sins as a means for righting wrongs in their lives. They found the good life was filled with joy and excitement. Their friends' lives were falling apart. They naturally drew other hurting people into their circle of healed persons. The church became "the place where I live."

At each point where new buildings were needed, the group was able to secure adequate facilities it could afford. Growth was not stopped by lack of space, nor was it hindered by heavy debt. They provided adequate space for their group as it developed. They did not build buildings significantly larger than their current size, so the space always seemed happily filled. It is particularly important that a building feel full as much as possible throughout the development stage. Building a building for the future is important, but plans should be made for intermediate stages which do not discourage the group.

A church never develops in a static situation. The community is always in growth or decline. Change is constant. As more affluent people moved into the community, the pastor was aware of the change and made attempts to reach these people as well as the original families of the area.

Several important bridge persons appeared at a critical time. The commander's wife and her family enjoyed working-class people who were of a different socioeconomic background. She, therefore, was quite comfortable with the original group. She also was able to identify with more affluent people who were moving into the area. The pastor's concern to reach the total community was learned by the congregation or may have been shared from the beginning. Therefore, they were more open to a wider variety of socioeconomic groups within their congregation than ordinarily might be expected. A church can reach a greater diversity of persons in its family if it has decided to try to reach everyone. Often churches are limited in size because they cannot bridge into more than one socioeconomic group. The appearance of bridge people, as well as the pastor who can be comfortable with a wide spread of diverse socioeconomic groups, was critical to the development of the church. The pastor, because of his education and experience, had personally been a part of several different socioeconomic groups. As a bridge person, he could communicate with a broader group of people than sometimes is possible.

The church had another advantage in that it was the first church of any denomination to be built in that community. If Baptists can determine the direction of growth in a city and start new churches in the path of that growth, as this church did, we can significantly change our success rate. It is also possible to start new churches in areas where churches already exist if one can find the vacuum left by the existing churches. Vacancies might occur in socioeconomic groups, personality types of pastors, the number of people present who prefer a small-church experience or the large volume of population who would require several medium-sized churches to reach. All of these vacancies would indicate new church needs.

Another critical quality that the pastor demonstrated at appropriate times was his ability to solve problems. For example, he decided to hold Sunday School classes in the homes of the teachers. The children could be brought to those homes for Sunday School by their parents. Then the teachers would bring them to the worship service to rejoin their parents. This was continued as long as Sunday School space was unavailable. The pastor might not have added the extra units that were needed if he had not solved the space problem. Space was a constant recurring need for the growing church. At each phase, the group was able to come up with temporary solutions and long-term plans.

The pastor also had a number of people-helping concepts. Even though he sometimes did not have the technical skills to help individuals, he felt love and friendship made a real difference. People were helped even if he had to refer them to more technically-equipped professionals to deal with their crisis. In other words, nobody ever presented a need who was turned away or not helped in some way.

The pastor also feels that the church's humble beginnings and inadequate facilities contributed to their staying with the basics in worship style. He feels staying with the basics—such as a simple sermon, music, Bible reading, and group participation—produced an attractive worship.

Finally, Pastor Bruce adequately demonstrated that starting a new church is not a mysterious operation. He simply lived one day at a time, working diligently from the needs of one person to another. He never had a course in church planting. He just found some way to use his good church experience and common sense. Many new churches are not started because sponsoring-church pastors fear they do not really know how to start a new church and help it grow. Pastor Bruce proved this fear is groundless. Church-starting courses are now common in seminaries and numerous books have been written, this one included. However, starting new churches is not as difficult as one might imagine. This case study demonstrates how ordinary daily acts of faith finally produce a spectacular miracle, the birth of a new church.

From this fruit stand . . .

. . . To this feed house . . .

**. . . To this $60,000 church—
Fort Foote Baptist Church**